THE GREAT ONE

"Gretzky [has given] people a whole new dimension to talk about."
—Al Strachan, *Toronto Globe & Mail*

"I know everything's been written about [him] . . . none of it is adequate."
—Bobby Clarke, Philadelphia Flyers

"What can he do for an encore?"
—Mark Messier, Edmonton Oilers

"Without him, the Oilers are out of it. With him, they win."
—John Davidson, New York Rangers (1979)

"Like Michael Jordan and John McEnroe, Gretzky is bigger than his sport."
—David Kottkamp, marketing director, Nike

"All I can do is my best and hope it's good enough."
—Wayne Gretzky

WAYNE
GRETZKY

Stephen
Hanks

A 2M COMMUNICATIONS LTD.
PRODUCTION

ST. MARTIN'S PRESS/NEW YORK

To my parents, for creating an environment in my youth that was the writer's equivalent of the backyard hockey rink.

To my brother Barry, who was one helluva sock-hockey goalie.

And to young hockey fans everywhere, who want and need heroes.

The writer would like to express his thanks to Madeleine Morel for her support and patience, Tom Olofson of St. Martin's Press, and the Los Angeles Kings publicity department. Very special thanks to my friend Stan Fischler, without whose help, guidance, and superior hockey knowledge this book wouldn't have been possible.

WAYNE GRETZKY

Photo research by Amanda Rubin.
Cover photograph by Focus on Sports.

ISBN: 0-312-91779-1   Can. ISBN: 0-312-91780-5

Printed in the United States of America

First St. Martin's Press mass market edition/February 1990

10 9 8 7 6 5 4 3 2 1

1

The Great One

WHEN TALKING ABOUT the world's superior athletes, just uttering a nickname can conjure up images of greatness. "The Babe," of course, was baseball's Babe Ruth. "The Shoe" was horse racing's Willie Shoemaker. "Johnny U" was football quarterback Johnny Unitas, and "Dr. J" was basketball legend Julius Erving. Boxing's Joe Louis was known as "The Brown Bomber" and golfing's Jack Nicklaus is called "The Golden Bear." Sometimes just one name says it all: "Pele"—"Martina"—"Ali."

But rarely does an athlete come along who so thoroughly dominates his sport, who is so far superior to his peers, who so clearly belongs at the apex of the pantheon, that we refer to him as if he were larger than life, like some ancient Egyptian pharaoh. There is one such athlete in our midst today, and we simply call him, "The Great One." Otherwise, he goes by the name of Wayne Gretzky.

Not yet thirty years of age, Wayne Gretzky has already become the greatest hockey player ever. Going into his 11th National Hockey League season in 1989–90, he had already turned the NHL record book into his autobiography. He has won the Hart Trophy as the league's Most Valuable Player in nine of his ten NHL seasons, and he holds or shares over 50 league records. The greatest of all those records was achieved six games into the '89–90 season when he surpassed the legendary Gordie Howe as the NHL's all-time scoring leader with 1851 points. But what made Gretzky's breaking of his boyhood idol's record even more remarkable is that he accomplished it playing 987 *fewer* games than Howe.

And Gretzky has parlayed all this greatness into becoming one of the world's richest athletes. His current deal with the Los Angeles Kings, who acquired Wayne from the Edmonton Oilers—a trade that shook up all of Canada—prior to the 1988–89 season, pays him approximately $2 million per season. *(USA Today* calculated that Gretzky made $37,037.03 per goal in '88–89). Such riches have enabled him to purchase a two and a half acre, $3 million estate in Encino Hills, California, and a cream-colored convertible Rolls-Royce for his wife, actress Janet Jones, in which to deal with Hollywood traffic.

It has been quite a heady climb for the kid who first tried on hockey skates at the age of two on a homemade rink outside his family's modest Brantford, Ontario abode. By age five Gretzky was already displaying the genius that would make him the ultimate hockey prodigy. His first goal was scored in a game against nine- and ten-year-olds. By age seven he was being called "the next Bobby Orr." At that time Orr was considered the greatest defenseman in hockey history. A year later came Gretzky's first 100-plus goal season, and two years later, at age ten, he scored an amazing 378 goals in a novice league. *Sports Illustrated* (which would eventually feature him on its cover ten times by the summer of 1989) had begun tracking his every rush up ice, and when he was eleven, Gretzky's idol Gordie Howe saw him and simply said, "God, he's got talent."

Such a comment is still a vast understatement nearly twenty years later. "Talent" is not quite enough of a word to describe what it is Wayne Gretzky has. All professional athletes have talent. Very few transcend their sport to the point of redefining it. Athletes like Gretzky don't just perform in a sport, they become a sport unto themselves. You can count the number of Gretzky's athletic genius peers in other sports on one hand; there's basketball's Michael Jordan, baseball/football player Bo Jackson, boxing champion Mike Tyson, diver Greg Louganis, and that's about it.

What distinguishes Gretzky from those superb sportsmen is not just that he has dominated his sport so completely, but that he's done it despite not being a particularly great physical specimen. At six feet, 170 pounds, Gretzky appears scrawny and unimposing compared to the 180 to 220 pound bruisers that play professional hockey today. You won't find bulging biceps or thunderous thighs on this guy. And compared to the skills of the great players of the past, Gretzky doesn't have as hard a slapshot as did Bobby Hull, he doesn't skate with the speed that made Guy Lafleur a legend, or stickhandle with the quickness and finesse that once made Bobby Orr the game's most gifted player.

Gretzky performs all those skills on an expert level, to be sure. He moves down a rink in a deceptively fast glide and in his silver and black Los Angeles Kings uniform, he can look like a Stealth Bomber trying to skate through, undetected by defensive radar. He shoots the puck with hands quicker than a magician's, handles the stick as if it were an extension of his arm, and passes with the accuracy of an Olympic-caliber archer.

But what sets The Great One apart from anybody who's ever played the game are his incredible hockey instincts and a seemingly superhuman sense of anticipation. While the speed of hockey almost dictates that every player develop a third eye, Gretzky plays as if he has eyes everywhere on his body. He also seems to exist in all three time dimensions. He knows where every player is on the ice at a given time, and has a feel not only for where the puck is now and where it came from, but where it is going.

"What amazes me most is that he never stops amazing me," one-time Edmonton Oilers teammate Mark Messier has said about Gretzky. "He'll do some totally incredible thing and you think, 'Okay, that's it; I'll never see the likes of that again.' Then, damn, he does something even more incredible."

One example of Messier's observation came during a stretch in December 1981. In consecutive games Gretzky produced three, two, one, and four-goal nights. "What can he do for an encore?" Messier thought. Gretzky showed him in the next game against the Philadelphia Flyers. He scored *five* goals. After the game Flyer captain Bobby Clarke (now the team's general manager) visited the Oiler locker room. "I know everything's been written about you," Clarke told Gretzky. "I think none of it is adequate."

Words to describe Gretzky's ability aren't

only inadequate, they often can't be uttered because his incredible talent leaves people with their mouths agape. One indescribable Gretzky specialty is the way he sets up in the ten-foot area behind the opposition goal to quarterback the offense.

"His passing from behind the net is uncanny," a rival NHL coach has observed. "He's the only player I've ever seen who can consistently center the puck from there through three sets of skates—and softly."

Gretzky has also mastered the art of passing the puck *over* the net. In one game early in his career Gretzky caught a pass from the side of the opposition goal, about four or five feet in the air, knocked it down, and all in one motion, backhanded a 12-foot shot that went over the goalie's left shoulder by about four or five inches.

"Everyone in the arena was stunned at that play," said Bryan Watson, a former coach of Gretzky's at Edmonton. "In practice the next day the first thing I do is call all the guys together and yell, 'Instant replay.' I tell the goalie to go into the net and see if Wayne can repeat that play. Everyone says, 'No way.' But Wayne takes the pass from the defenseman, knocks it down, and makes the shot almost the exact way."

Gretzky can use the opposing goal as a shield, a screen, even as a teammate. During a game against the New York Rangers in December 1988, Gretzky had possession of the puck behind the New York goal when two Rangers skated toward him. With a flick of the wrist he banked the puck off the bottom back of the goal and received a pass from himself. Then he got pinned along the boards by the New York defensemen but still skated away with the puck. "He looks like he's playing for the Harlem Globetrotters of hockey," observed Ranger broadcaster John Davidson.

But no great athlete can perform based on sheer instinct. From the moment he laced on skates, Wayne's father Walter instilled in his son the practice-makes-perfect ethic. Even after winning his first NHL Most Valuable Player award at age nineteen, Gretzky was not above working to improve his game. Despite a 51-goal season, Wayne felt that he had failed to score on a high percentage of breakaways, those opportunities where the goalie is the last line of defense against a player's rush up the ice. So all that summer he worked with his brothers Keith, Glenn, and Brett, in front of the family's garage with a net on the pavement and a tennis ball. As Bryan Watson put it: "How many players with 51 goals the season before would do that?"

And how many superstar athletes, with packed appointment books, would devote as much time to charitable causes as Wayne Gretzky has since becoming a world-renowned superstar? Not many. Although he may now make millions representing major corporations like Nike, General Mills, and Nissan, he has also raised thousands by sponsoring tennis and golf tournaments for the National Institute for the Blind in Canada and organizations aiding the mentally handicapped.

Gretzky has also become hockey's greatest promoter. On December 12, 1988, headlines in sports sections of the New York papers blared, GRETZKY COMES TO HARLEM. On the morning after a night game in Long Island, The Great One led a group of NHL players to a rink in Central Park, where they taught hockey to some Black and Latin ghetto children.

"It's been a while since I've skated outdoors, and this is the oddest place I've ever practiced," Gretzky told a bunch of writers gathered for the occasion. "But I've always said that in order for this game to grow, we're going to need new places in the United States. You've got to start somewhere."

The Great One had a grand old time at the great park. Despite freezing temperatures, he stayed long after the clinic, signing autographs for over 200 people, exchanging high-fives with the budding hockey players, and flinging his stick to a kid in the crowd. "He's the only one I know," said a youngster, pointing to the man wearing the famous number 99. As Gretzky left the rink he noticed two kids battling for a loose puck as if a Stanley Cup championship were on the line.

"Hey, hey, don't get hurt out there," advised Gretzky. "You guys are the NHL stars of the future."

For the present, however, Wayne Gretzky is THE NHL star. Sure, some hockey experts are making a case, and a good one, that the Pittsburgh Penguins' Mario Lemieux is now the league's best player. But Gretzky, who is as approachable, intelligent, witty, and articulate as any athlete in pro sports, clearly holds the title of Mr. Hockey in the United States and Canada. There isn't another player in the game who would be invited to host NBC-TV's *Saturday Night Live* as Gretzky was last spring. And given that the sport has had few marquee names in the last decade, many people feel that Gretzky has saved the NHL. In a February 1989 column in *Esquire*, the magazine referred to Gretzky as "Hockey's Only Hope." And as a writer put it in a national hockey publication a couple of years back: "It seems that for the past nine years Wayne Gretzky has always been there when needed to wipe scrambled egg off the face of an embarrassed league."

Gretzky takes his role as a league spokesman very seriously. An NHL general manager once pointed out that, rightly or wrongly, Gretzky feels he is responsible for the league's image. After all, the NHL practically anointed

Gretzky as some kind of savior as soon as he arrived from the defunct World Hockey Association in 1979. At that point there were only three or four competitive NHL teams—the Montreal Canadiens, the Boston Bruins, and the New York Islanders—and with the exception of Montreal's Guy Lafleur, there were no larger-than-life hockey stars selling the sport in the United States.

This was also the period in NHL history when fighting and violence were rampant throughout the league, thanks primarily to an intensely aggressive style popularized by the Philadelphia Flyers, who were known as the "Broad Street Bullies." It sometimes seemed as if the words "hockey" and "violence" were synonymous. When TV sportscasters showed hockey highlights, fans saw more shots of flying fists than pucks hitting twine. The most popular sports joke became, "I went to a fight last night and a hockey game broke out."

Then a nineteen-year-old phenom named Gretzky burst onto the NHL scene, scored 51 goals, and led the league in assists and points. "The NHL needs something to hang its hat on," said Gordie Howe as he watched the kid dazzle the hockey world, "and Gretzky looks like a hat tree."

"Wayne entered the scene just at the right time and took the attention away from fighting," said Al Strachan, the hockey columnist for the *Toronto Globe & Mail.* "Suddenly people were wondering if this kid was for real, and they were following him as his stats piled up. Here was a guy who didn't have to fight, but could go the length of the rink with the puck; who could find tiny holes in the defense. Gretzky gave people a whole new dimension to talk about, something other than fighting. He brought hockey into a different era."

The Wayne Gretzky era of the NHL is now skating into its second decade and shows no sign of ending any time soon. This is the story of his first ten NHL years and everything else that has led up to the reign of "The Great One."

2
The Child Prodigy

THERE WAS THIS EVENING a few years back when Walter Gretzky was driving to his home in Brantford, Ontario, after a day of work at the Canadian Bell Telephone Company. As he turned into his driveway he saw a large object blocking his path into the garage. The object was something Walter Gretzky had always dreamed about owning. It was a big, black Cadillac. Where could this car have come from? Did somebody park in his driveway by mistake? Walter Gretzky saw that his license number was on the plates. It turned out that the car was a present from his hockey superstar son Wayne, who at that point in his career had been awarded so many automobiles he could have started his own dealership.

The gift was just another expression of thanks from a son to a father who had done everything in his power to grease his boy's road to stardom. Like many other dads who had failed to accomplish their dream, Walter Gretzky spent every spare moment seeing to it that his son would have a better chance. The highest the elder Gretzky ever reached in hockey was the Junior B level. But if Walter didn't possess the innate ability to make the NHL, maybe his first son, Wayne, would. If the son had any God-given gifts at all, they would be enhanced by the father's knowledge and dedication, and maybe, just maybe, it might mean Wayne could achieve what is the ultimate to millions of Canadian boys—a career in the National Hockey League.

When Walter Gretzky first exposed his two-year-old son to hockey games on television, he couldn't have yet known that his genes had produced a prodigy. At an age when most children are still coping with balancing on their feet, Wayne was sliding up and down his parents' living room floor, imitating the people he was seeing on the television.

On Saturdays Walter would take his wife Phyllis and son Wayne to grandmother Gretzky's for a visit. After dinner, with Mary Gretzky ensconced in her favorite chair, her little grandson would knock a rubber ball around the room with a ministick, trying to get the "puck" though her goalposts, er, legs. "I think," Mary Gretzky once said, "I was the only goalie to stop him."

The unrestrained joy on his son's face as he tried to maneuver a ball through his grandmother's limbs was all Walter Gretzky had to see. Soon Wayne was being fitted for tiny ice skates and Walter was building a 22-by-45-foot rink behind the Gretzky house. Before long the two-year-old, standing unsupported on the ice with a stick, was being instilled with the philosophies of sound hockey and the importance of practice. These early father-and-son work sessions would last well into the evening. "They'd stay out there real late," Phyllis Gretzky once recalled, "and sometimes Walter would stay out longer than Wayne."

If Walter Gretzky was becoming obsessed with his son's training, it was because he saw the potential immediately. Wayne was an example of those stories Walter had heard about famous talents who just happened to have such a genius for something, they could make the doing of it seem effortless. Like George Gershwin, who could play the piano before he took one lesson. Or Judy Garland, who as a child could belt out a tune as if she were a professional singer. Walter wanted to give birth to a son who would learn to become a good hockey player. What he got was a son who was born to play hockey.

No drill was too difficult for Walter Gretzky's little boy. By the time he was five, Wayne was skating around pylons that Walter had positioned strategically on the ice. Wayne would have to skate and stickhandle the puck around them. Later Wayne would enjoy relating how "my father had me doing drills like that long before the Soviets made such a big deal out of them."

"The pylon drills were great in developing puck possession, which is one of the most important aspects in hockey," explained Walter years later. "Pylons and practice make perfect. The amazing thing, though, was that Wayne never got tired of skating around those pylons."

As Wayne mastered each drill, Walter increased the degree of difficulty. Now when Wayne had eluded the pylons, he would have to aim the puck for little rings placed in each corner of the net or shoot through narrow holes in a picnic table placed in front of the goal. Once his son became comfortable performing such drills, Walter Gretzky began teaching Wayne how to think on the ice. The great knack Wayne has for anticipating and diagnosing a play—an ability that fans believe comes quite natural to Gretzky—has its roots in those early backyard-rink practice sessions.

"I always told Wayne that if you want to play hockey, you've got to do something the big guys can't do," Walter Gretzky said. "One thing you can do is outthink them. And you can maneuver like a magician with the puck. At a very young age he was told, 'Don't go where the puck's been, go where it's going to be.' "

Walter also instilled in his son an appreciation for the work ethic. On those rare occasions when Wayne didn't feel like practicing, Walter would tell him, "Fine, just be prepared to get up at seven every morning and go to work when you grow up." He also encouraged Wayne and his younger children—daughter Kim and sons Keith, Glenn, and Brent—to get involved in track and field because Walter felt track built self-discipline and confidence. (Kim, in fact, became the Ontario Dominion champion in the 100-, 200-, and 400-meter dashes). But was Walter Gretzky putting too much pressure on his eldest son? Was he becoming the sports version of a stage mother, or one of those obnoxious parents you find at Little League games all over America?

"I don't think I pushed any of my kids into sport," Walter once told *Edmonton Journal* writer Terry Jones. "But I told them that when they go into a sport, I believed they shouldn't give it a half effort. Some people may say that's pushing. But I believe when you go into sport, you have to try to do the best that you can, all the time. I don't believe in the philosophy that in minor hockey the kids should just be sent out to have fun. If the boy is sent out to do the best he can, and he does it, he's going to be happy."

After three years of intense personal training from his father, Wayne Gretzky was ready to play organized hockey. But instead of starting out in the novice division with the youngest boys, Wayne was skilled enough at five to play in the Novice A division, one which usually didn't accept players until they'd reached their tenth birthday. Naturally, Wayne excelled immediately. In his second season for the Nadrofsky Steelers, he scored 27 goals. Between ages seven and eight the amazing kid scored an amazing 104 goals, and though Wayne mostly played defense, he did everything but play goalie.

Whenever one of Wayne's teams needed a goal, he would be placed at a forward spot and hardly ever got a breather. During one particular game during those early years, he was inserted in a contest his team was trailing 3–0 with little time remaining in the third period. After a brief rest on the bench, Wayne was told by his coach to get the team back into the game. Gretzky did that and more—he tied it up himself in less than a minute.

Young Wayne Gretzky was developing a pattern that would continue into his professional career—that of always seeming able to top himself. During the 1970–71 season, playing for minor and major novice teams, he scored 196 goals. But that was only a prelude for even more phenomenal accomplishments. The next season—his final as a novice player, and during which he was between nine and ten—he scored an unbelievable 378 goals and had all of the Canadian media following him around. National networks and publications enthusiastically recorded his exploits.

"The scoring feats of ten-year-old Wayne Gretzky of Brantford," read one story out of Ontario, "are posing a pleasant problem for organizers of the Brampton novice tournament. The four-foot-four, seventy-pound dynamo has been turning them away at the doors here and didn't disappoint his fans again Wednesday night, scoring nine goals and assisting on two others in Brantford's 12–2 win over Sault Ste. Marie . . ."

And the media were also anxious to record his every word. "I want to be the next Gordie Howe," Wayne told reporters, even though Boston Bruin defenseman Bobby Orr was the hero of the day. "Bobby Orr doesn't have as many tricks as Gordie Howe."

But with all this early adulation came the inevitable backlash and the pressure that goes with it. While Walter, a camera buff, filmed his son's highs on the ice, he also had to deal with the lows Wayne experienced off of it. Teammates and opponents began resenting the special treatment afforded to Wayne at the expense of other kids. Rumors circulated that Wayne Gretzky was an arrogant snob whom the referees protected on the ice. "You knew if you took a run at him," recalled an opposing player from the novice league days, "someone would flatten you."

Walter wasn't immune to criticism, either. There was one game in 1972 when Wayne scored all the team's goals in a 5–4 defeat. But after the contest a parent on Wayne's team was heard to say, "Sure, he might have scored four, but he cost us five."

"When I would coach Wayne, some of the parents would say I was favoring him," recalled Walter. "And they would call him a puck hog, a one-man team, and would blame him when his team lost. It's only human nature that people would resent Wayne for scoring 200 or 300 goals in a season. If your boy is on that team, you're not going to be happy. But many was the time I saw him crying, and after that big season when he was ten, the fun starting leaving the game for him."

But Walter Gretzky's kid was feisty and knew how and when to stand up for himself. The season after he scored the 378 goals, the coach of his first major peewee team told him there was no place for "hot dogs" on his squad. As Wayne remembered it, "I had gotten 120 assists that season, too, and this guy was telling me I was a hot dog." It had also been the year Gordie Howe had retired, and Wayne's new hero was Gilbert Perreault, the flashy star of the Buffalo Sabres. The same peewee coach told Wayne he didn't want any Gilbert Perreaults on his team, either. "I told him," recalled Gretzky, "if Gilbert Perreault is such a hot dog, why is he playing in the NHL and on Team Canada in the series against the Soviet Union, while you're coaching in this league?"

Wayne scored 295 goals during his two peewee hockey seasons. And when he registered his 1000th "career" goal on April 10, 1974, it rated big headlines in the Ontario newspapers. But Wayne was getting tired of the subtle abuse directed toward him in Brantford, and he was becoming impatient with the inferior competition. The Canadian hometown was just too small a place for a player of Wayne Gretzky's large talent, ability that needed constant nourishment if it was to continue blossoming. But prospects for improvement seemed gloomy, and in this most depressing time of his childhood, Wayne often thought about giving up the game he loved.

But quitting was never a viable option. What the prodigy needed was a change of scenery, and the very competitive Metropolitan Toronto Hockey League was interested in his considerable talents. Wayne certainly believed he was ready for the big city, but naturally, Walter wasn't quite convinced his fourteen-year-old was prepared to spend months away from home. He knew his son was shy and quiet, the kind of kid who kept his feelings inside. There were other factors that were telling Walter Gretzky to keep his child in Brantford, like the kind of negative influences that exist in any big-city environment. In the minds of Walter and Phyllis Gretzky, their son would be exposed to things he'd never experienced before—things like crime, alcohol, and drugs.

Wayne understood his parents' fears, but he came up with the best possible argument to convince them he could handle the move. The Gretzkys listened intently during a family discussion as Wayne told them that it was just as easy to get alcohol and drugs in Brantford as it would be in Toronto. The only high Wayne Gretzky wanted was the one he achieved by performing on the ice. Walter Gretzky now knew his son was mature and responsible enough to handle Toronto. Besides, the cosmopolitan atmosphere might help bring Wayne out of his shell at a time when he would have to be on his guard. Once in Toronto, Wayne would be besieged by coaches, scouts, agents, anybody who would try to manipulate the prodigy for their own gain.

Wayne was hoping for peace and harmony in Toronto and a chance to simply concentrate on his game. But even this quest was halted like a goalie stopping one of his break-aways. As Gretzky was preparing to play for a bantam league in Toronto, the Ontario Minor Hockey Association announced they wouldn't release Gretzky to play in the Metropolitan Toronto Hockey League. When Wayne scored two goals in his initial bantam game, the OMHA suspended him, even after a Toronto family, the Cornishes, made Wayne their legal ward. When the Gretzkys' appeal of Wayne's suspension was denied, the prodigy was forced to play for a team that could use play-ers from anywhere in Canada.

As it turned out, the battle between the two leagues could have been a blessing in dis-guise for the budding superstar. Now he was playing with the Toronto Young Nationals of the Metro Junior B Hockey League, which in-cluded players as old as twenty. And as he had all through his young life, Wayne excelled playing against experienced competition. At the end of the season he was voted the league's Rookie of the Year, and everyone who had seen him play on this level sensed the same thing—that they were watching the de-velopment of a future NHL star.

3

The Teenage Superstar

MAYBE IT WAS HOMESICKNESS. Maybe it was the raging hormones of a fifteen-year-old. Maybe it was the superior competition. Maybe it was the relentless pressure to perform better than he had the game before. Whatever it was, at the beginning of the 1976–77 season, his second with the Toronto Young Nationals, Wayne Gretzky experienced his first slump.

During many games, he skated as though he had all the energy of a car low on gas. He would appear exhausted as he sat on the bench waiting for his next shift, and even Walter Gretzky was concerned enough to think his son might have mononucleosis.

It was possible that athletically Wayne

had spread himself too thin. Besides playing Junior B hockey, Gretzky was running cross-country and playing midget basketball for West Humber Collegiate Institute in Etobicoke. While he was just above average as a runner, he was the best basketball player on the team, averaging 20 points a game for a club that regularly scored about 40, and leading them to the championship. Like a hockey player who enjoyed rushing the puck the length of the ice, Wayne liked driving to the hoop in a basketball game.

"He wasn't the best basketball player I ever coached," recalled Charlie Simpson, Gretzky's coach at West Humber, "but he was the best natural athlete. What I really remember about those days, though, is Wayne being bothered by the other team's swearing. It made him genuinely upset."

Wayne was even more perturbed when in late December the ranking of hockey players eligible for the midget-age draft to a higher league was released. Gretzky scanned the list and saw his name below that of 183 other players in the country.

Besides Walter Gretzky, one man who tried to ignore Wayne's lackluster play and subsequent low ranking was Gus Badali, a budding player agent. Badali first caught Gretzky's act while watching Gordie Howe's son Murray playing for the Young Nats. Sure, Badali had heard about Wayne's exploits in

Brantford, but now he was seeing the much-heralded youngster firsthand, and was not impressed. But Badali, a former Junior B player and coach, knew hockey talent. "Even though Wayne wasn't playing particularly well that season," Badali recalled, "it was obvious he was something special. There was something about him that made you realize someday he'd be great."

Gus Badali sought out Walter Gretzky. What a coup it would be, the novice agent must have thought, if my first client was a player with the potential to be the best ever. Walter was impressed with Badali's knowledge and his easygoing manner, and besides, Gordie Howe's boys were Badali's friends. Walter Gretzky agreed to let Badali represent his son's interests.

Right around Christmas, Wayne started playing well again, as if Santa had left Gretzky's game under the tree. Wayne's performance peaked during the Ontario Hockey Association Junior B playoffs, when he scored 73 points in 23 games. In one playoff contest he scored four goals and an assist in the final ten minutes of a 7–6 victory. Overall, he finished second in the league in scoring. The scouts were drooling again, his ranking soared, and when the Junior A draft arrived in June, the Sault Ste. Marie Greyhounds made Wayne the third player in the nation selected. Wayne was cool at first to the idea of playing in the western Ontario town, preferring to flaunt his talents for the Peterborough Petes, a team closer to home. But after visiting the hometown of NHL superstars Phil and Tony Esposito on the banks of the St. Mary's River, Gretzky and Badali decided they wouldn't be blue in "the Soo."

It didn't take long for Wayne to prove that his advance billing wasn't just hype. In his very first game for the Greyhounds, he was a thoroughbred, notching three goals and three assists in a 6–1 victory. With each Gretzky appearance, attendance at the Sault Ste. Marie games increased, until it had doubled to 2500 per game. Wayne was even more of a drawing card when the Greyhounds hit the road. Ottawa, Peterborough, and Hamilton all boasted their largest crowds of the season when he was in town.

Settling in as the Greyhounds' number-one center, Wayne put on a spectacular show that even impressed his teammates. They'd all heard the stories about the prodigious-scoring prodigy from Brantford, but couldn't believe they could all be true, especially after seeing how relatively normal the kid appeared. He wasn't big, he wasn't strong, he wasn't fast. Greyhounds coach Muzz Mac-Pherson thought the scrawny kid "would get killed in junior," and Gretzky himself thought he was so slow on the ice, he referred to his skating as being "brutal." But after one practice the Greyhounds believed.

"I'll never forget that first practice," recalled MacPherson. "Gretz skated up to me and asked me how many points our top scorer had the year before. I told him 178, and he said, 'Oh, that's no problem. I'll break that.' He wasn't cocky, just confident." Marveled Paul Mancini, who played on Wayne's line that season, "He did things in that first practice we'd never seen before."

And when people would bring up Gretzky's deficiencies to Angelo Bumbacco, a veteran observer of junior hockey, and Sault Ste. Marie's general manager, he would simply say: "People told me the same thing about Phil Esposito that they tell me about Wayne Gretzky—that he can't skate. I tell them they're absolutely right. He can't skate a lick. All he can do is score goals."

Like all great goal-scorers, Wayne was also criticized for lacking defensive ability, a talent rarely in abundance among sixteen-year-old junior hockey players. E. M. Swift, a *Sports Illustrated* writer who in an article that season called Gretzky "Canada's answer to young superstars Steve Cauthen and Nadia Comaneci," told a local reporter that defensively Gretzky had a long way to go. When Wayne scored a goal the next day and had two assists in a 4–2 win, he walked by Swift and said, "Good enough defense for you?" Even

Swift had to admit "he was flawless in his own end all night."

As if Wayne Gretzky wasn't standing out enough in every game he played, he also became the only player in all of hockey to wear number 99. Wayne really wanted to don number 9, the one worn by his idol Gordie Howe (and also hockey legends Maurice Richard and Bobby Hull) and one he had worn during his youth hockey career. When he found the number was taken he tried wearing numbers 14 and 19, but discarded them because "the ones didn't feel right on my back." Greyhound coach MacPherson came up with a unique solution to the kid's problem. He suggested Gretzky wear number 99, which Wayne ultimately made one of the most famous numbers in sports history. "That was the year Phil Esposito and Ken Hodge were traded from the Boston Bruins to the New York Rangers," MacPherson explained. "Rod Gilbert (the Rangers' superstar) already had number seven, so Phil took 77 and Hodge took 88. I figured if they could do it, Gretz could go from nine to 99. He was gonna be a marked man anyway."

What MacPherson feared was that because of Gretzky's talent and reputation, he would be subject to opposition cheap shots, and those fears turned out to be well-founded. Three times during the season Wayne was forced to the hospital for postgame X rays after receiving stick slashes from players trying to stop his elusive moves.

"It scares me to think there might be some big son of a gun who is just out there on the ice to try to get me out of the game," Gretzky told E. M. Swift of *Sports Illustrated*. "Guys are always telling me that the next time I touch the puck, they're going to stuff their sticks down my throat. What can you do? You've got to go ahead and tough it and hope they were kidding."

Wayne Gretzky was becoming such a phenomenon, he'd become a marked man to a different group—the media. He was not only profiled in *Sports Illustrated,* but also in the *New York Times* and big Canadian publications like *Weekend* and *Maclean's.* Such an intense media onslaught can be more than a lot of professionals can bear, but Gretzky seemed to be as natural around pens and cameras as around face-off circles and goal creases.

"Since I was six years old," Wayne once explained, "I've had a lot of media attention. I was brought up to believe that when people are interested in you, you have a responsibility to them, that you have to watch what you say and do whenever you're in the public eye."

Wayne had a major input in shaping his own legend, which was continuing to grow as that first season in the Soo progressed. He was the youngest player on the Canadian national junior team competing in the world tournament that Christmas. In front of thousands of fans in Montreal, Wayne topped all scorers with eight goals and nine assists in six games, was the only Canadian player named to the tourney all-star squad, and was named the best center over Bobby Smith of Ottawa, who would become the NHL's first draft choice that June.

And those honors were just the beginning during Wayne Gretzky's first teenage superstar season. He set a Greyhound record with 70 goals and 182 points, finishing second in the league scoring race to Smith, who also beat out Wayne as the first-team All-Star center. Gretzky set a league record for most goals and points in a season by a rookie and, naturally, won the league Rookie of the Year award. He also led the league with seven shorthanded goals, 21 multiple-goal games, and seven hat tricks (three-goal games). In the league's annual coaches' poll Wayne was unanimously voted the league's "smartest player," and also received the coaches' acclaim as the "most dangerous in the goal area," and "best playmaker." In the league playoffs, Wayne led all players with 20 assists in 13 games. And on top of all that, the league recognized his sportsmanship by giving him an award as "the most gentlemanly player."

If there was a downside to the season for Wayne, it was being apart from his dad for long stretches of time. While he was playing for Sault Ste. Marie, he lived with a man named Jim Bodnar and his wife Sylvia, who were old friends of his parents. Jim Bodnar was able to get a close-up view of the unique relationship between Wayne and Walter Gretzky.

"I don't think you could be any more loyal than Walter," Bodnar told the *Edmonton Sun.* "He gives everything he has to his kids. I remember one time Walter couldn't get a game on the radio, so he called and had us hold the mouthpiece to the radio. They didn't get up to too many games, because Walter just couldn't afford it. He had this old car, but he couldn't put money in it. Because of that, he and Wayne were always on the phone, discussing strategy, talking about what Wayne was doing. They both seemed to know something special was happening."

While the name of Wayne Gretzky was becoming famous throughout the hockey world, Gus Badali was making a big name for himself as an agent. Despite the fact that the National Hockey League and the six-year-old upstart World Hockey Association had an agreement with Junior leagues not to draft players before their Junior careers were over at twenty, Badali was securing six-figure contracts with WHA teams for "underage" Juniors. Capitalizing on the new league's intense desire to establish its credibility in the hockey world, Badali made deals for promising young pros like Wayne Dillon (with the Toronto Toros), John Tonelli (with the Houston Aeros), and Mark Napier (with the Birmingham Bulls). Would Badali's most famous client be next to join the new league? Only a fool would think that the publicity-starved WHA wasn't salivating at the thought of grabbing a consensus future pro superstar like Gretzky. And if the new league did come courting him, was he ready to play professional hockey at seventeen years of age? Wayne didn't really think so. All he was thinking about was playing another year at the Soo for $75 a week.

"But after one more year, I'd be bored," Wayne admitted, while talk of turning pro swirled around him. "Mentally, I'm ready for the pros, but physically I'm not."

Gus Badali and those daring WHA owners, desperate for marquee-name drawing cards to strengthen their flamboyant investments, would ultimately be the judges of that.

4

The Young Millionaire

WHEN WAYNE GRETZKY was eight years old and playing in the Ontario peewee league playoffs, one of the opposing players was the son of millionaire entrepreneur and Canadian Football League team owner John F. Bassett. A few years after seeing Gretzky on the ice for the first time, Bassett would become the owner of the Birmingham Bulls franchise in the World Hockey Association, and by 1978 Bassett had talked often with Gus Badali about the players in his burgeoning stable. So it was only natural that Bassett would expect the first crack at signing hockey's latest sensation—Wayne Gretzky.

The WHA was a struggling league, but was proving to be an itch the established NHL couldn't scratch. Aging NHL superstars like Bobby Hull and Gordie Howe signed with WHA teams, causing an escalation of salaries in the NHL. Badali sensed that the WHA wouldn't last and that some of its franchises would ultimately be absorbed by the NHL. Figuring it would just be a matter of time when his high-profile client would be strutting his stuff in the NHL, Badali was anxious to seal a big WHA deal for Gretzky. And with the WHA signing underage juniors faster than a Hull slapshot (the NHL was abiding by the agreement), the question was not *if* Gretzky would be signed, but by who and for how much.

Bassett was expecting a Badali price pitch, and the agent threw it, but it was much higher than the $50,000 the Bulls' owner had spent on each of five other Junior players. The cost of Gretzky, Bassett told Badali, was too high for even his checkbook.

"I figured Gretzky would get hurt in the WHA," Bassett admitted to the *Toronto Star* in 1987. "He was a seventeen-year-old kid, terribly frail, and I thought the pros might kill him. I didn't want to be a party to it. Well, subsequent events have shown how stupid I was. That story is useful anytime I start thinking I'm a genius."

Bassett recommended Badali contact Vancouver-based entrepreneur Nelson Skalbania, who owned the WHA's struggling Indianapolis Racers franchise. Skalbania had been a partner of Peter Pocklington's with the Edmonton Oilers, but his own team wasn't proving nearly as successful, both on the ice and at the box office. Skalbania needed a name player to bring in fans and save his team, and he knew that Wayne Gretzky could be that name.

It was already approaching July, so Skalbania had to act fast or lose the kid to one of his equally hungry fellow owners. He called Badali and asked him to name a price. The number sounded pretty good to Nelson, and soon he was giving Badali a thousand dollars for plane fare to bring Wayne and his parents to Vancouver. After agreeing verbally to a deal, the Gretzkys hopped aboard Skalbania's private jet and signed a four-year guaranteed personal services contract for $875,000 while they were flying over Alberta. The deal also called for a three-year option and a $250,000 bonus with $50,000 in cash. "If he can't play hockey," joked Skalbania after the signing, "he's going to be the most expensive handball partner I've ever had."

Wayne Gretzky was now not only the youngest player in WHA history, but the youngest athlete in any team sport. Ironically, the oldest such player at that point was Wayne's idol Gordie Howe, who at fifty was skating for the New England Whalers. Nobody expected Gretzky to have to justify his decision—even rival-league general manager Harry Sinden understood, saying, "You can't blame the kid for getting a big offer and taking it"—but Wayne explained one of his motives for signing by saying, "I've got one semester of high school to go, and the only reason I could think of to stay in the Juniors was to graduate. But an offer like that is hard to turn down. I guess the master plan worked —the dream's come true. I never thought a player should be restricted from advancing because of his age. That's why I'm grateful to the WHA for giving me a chance to turn pro early."

"All my life people kept telling me I couldn't make it," he said on another occasion, after the deal was finalized. "If I'd listened I'd still be back in Brantford. All my life I've worked to become a professional hockey player. If I didn't take this opportunity, and broke a leg or something back in the Soo, it could be all over."

Skalbania wasted no time promoting his new star. He quoted stories like one in *Sports Illustrated* which said that Gretzky was "the most exciting player since the Montreal Canadiens' Guy Lafleur." He had Wayne make one promotional appearance after another. He organized "The Great Gretzky Fan Club." He told everyone how well-liked Gretzky was among his new teammates, who called him "Brinks" because of his huge contract. But soon the Racers' owner was second-guessing his most publicized business decision. Even with The Great Gretzky in tow, people in Indianapolis weren't buying hockey tickets.

"We had 2200 season-ticket holders when I signed him," Skalbania recalled for the *Edmonton Sun* in 1987. "A month later sales had skyrocketed all the way up to 2300. I guess everyone in Indianapolis who wanted to watch hockey had their tickets. The kid didn't make any difference at all."

Things didn't look much better to the owner once the 1978–79 season began. The joy of July had given way to the angst of October. Skalbania figured he needed an average of 11,800 fans at each Racer home game to keep his team afloat. But after an opening night crowd of 11,728—a high turnout due no doubt to curiosity about Gretzky—attendance dropped to between five and seven thousand for subsequent games. Gretzky could have been an anonymous member of an Indianapolis 500 pit crew for all people in the town apparently cared.

Skalbania became more nervous than a rookie goalie having to stop a penalty shot. With a million-dollar loss on the season staring at him from the balance sheet, and the prospect of his team not being included in the proposed NHL-WHA merger, Skalbania knew he had to unload the Gretzky contract. He tried peddling Wayne to Winnipeg, but the

Jets said no. So the desperate owner contacted his old partner, Peter Pocklington, who, according to Skalbania, "operated with an open checkbook."

Skalbania didn't waste any time. He moved faster on making a deal with Pocklington than he had four months earlier with the Gretzkys. On November 4 the Racers' owner sent Gretzky, winger Peter Driscoll, and goalie Eddie Mio to the Edmonton Oilers for approximately $850,000. (Years later, Mio would joke that "Pocklington paid $849,999.99 for Gretz and one cent for me and Driscoll. But I'm not complaining. My name will be associated with Wayne's forever. It's something no one can take away from me.") Wayne Gretzky's Indianapolis career had consisted of eight games, in which he notched three goals and three assists, but Pocklington was sure he was making a sound investment in the future.

"We feel that if we're going to be in the NHL," said the Oilers' owner after announcing the deal, "we need a superstar. And Wayne is going to be one."

In the meantime, the Racers' few season-ticket holders felt like they'd been hip-checked, slashed, and pummeled to the ice. Many suspected that Skalbania had always planned to get rid of Gretzky for a quick profit. Some fans even filed a class-action suit that went nowhere. The *Indianapolis Star* chipped in, ripping the owner with the head-

line, HEY NELSON, GO BACK TO SKALBANIA. Though
at the time he claimed to be pleased with the
deal, Skalbania's franchise was doomed along
with the others that wouldn't make the cut in
the merger deal with the NHL.

For his part, Wayne took all these mone-
tary machinations in stride, as he had almost
everything since his novice hockey days. At
the post-trade press conference he calmly told
Indianapolis fans that he was "sorry to be
leaving the Racers." Then, after stroking his
blond facial fuzz, he added, "But the Oilers
have shown faith in me, and I'd better produce."

And produce he did. In his first twelve
games for the Oilers, "The Great Gretzky," as
the Edmonton media officially dubbed him,
had six goals and eight assists. The Oilers
were 1–4 when Gretzky arrived, and went on
an 11–4 streak in their next fifteen games. He
was getting countless standing ovations for
his creative passing and fancy stickhandling;
and his skating, said to be the weak part of
his game as a Junior, was becoming effortless
and deceptive. As he approached his eighteenth birthday he had grown to six-feet, 170
pounds, and was developing more strength in
his legs. Wayne's new coach, Glen Sather, was
amazed by the skills of his new wunderkind.

"He has innate hockey sense, like all
great players," Sather told *Sports Illustrated*
that December. "Coming out of his end, he al-

ways seems in position to take the pass. And when he gets the puck he knows where everybody is, the way a center is supposed to. I hate to put this on him, but a player like Gretzky comes along only once every ten years. He's not up there with Orr, Hull, and Howe yet, but he's not far away, either."

But Sather, who was a NHL journeyman tough-guy during his playing career in the sixties, wasn't always enamored of Gretzky's play in the defensive end. In fact, he noticed the kid rarely came back behind his own blue line. When Gretzky made a first-period defensive mistake that led to a goal during a mid-December game against the Cincinnati Stingers, Sather benched him the rest of the period. After letting Wayne think about his bad play for a few minutes into the second period, Sather let him take his regular shift. Now, fired up as much as he had ever been since he began playing hockey, Gretzky scored a hat trick that turned a 2–1 Edmonton deficit into a 5–2 victory. The demanding Oiler coach was impressed.

"He could have pouted and sulked," Sather said after the game. "But he didn't, and that is a turning point in his career. Not just anyone could keep motivated with a contract like his. But he's confident as hell, and he firmly believes he's going to be the best player in the world."

Gretzky exhibited his desire to be the best

—every day in practice, where he would put on a show that would leave even his veteran teammates in awe. When he worked on deflecting shots from the point, he could direct the puck to any part of the net, like a pool player calling the pocket. He could even deflect some shots that would stop *on top* of the net. On one particular night before a game against Birmingham, Gretzky banked three pucks in a row into an empty net off the goalpost—from the other end of the rink. Then Gretzky took a teammate down the ice with him on a two-on-none rush. The teammate carried the puck down the right boards and, at Wayne's signal, sent a waist-high pass behind the streaking Gretzky. Without breaking stride, Wayne bent his leg behind him and deflected the pass off his skate and onto his stick. And he could make that incredible move more than once.

Fortunately for Wayne, at this point in his life it wasn't all practices, games, and media attention. He lived at the home of Jim Bodnar's brother Ray, where he watched a lot of hockey on TV, to study the other players, and served as the designated cleaner because he couldn't cook. "His favorite thing at our house was the microwave," recalled Bodnar. "I also remember that Wayne had a terrible memory. He'd leave little notes all over the house to remind himself what was important that day. But he was a wonderful house guest and we loved him like he was our own son."

Wayne drove around in a 1979 Thunderbird, but his allowance was so low that when he broke down and bought a plastic scraper for cleaning ice off the windshield, his teammates applauded. He also planned on attending high school after the season so he could get his diploma, and he began dating for the first time.

"When I'm twenty-three," Wayne told *Sports Illustrated,* "I don't want to look back and feel I missed being a teenager. I want to be a hockey player and a normal seventeen-year-old. People are always saying, 'Aren't you missing something playing hockey?' The way I look at it, I'm not missing anything, I'm getting extra."

Wayne couldn't have known just how much extra he would be getting as his eighteenth birthday approached. When it arrived on January 26, Pocklington put on a party even a parent would have trouble topping. A ceremony was held at center ice in Edmonton's Northlands Coliseum and a cake in the shape of a 99 was wheeled out. Then Wayne was given some presents. And what presents! The appetizer was a bottle of sparkling Baby Duck champagne from his teammates, who were anxious to see baby Gretz take his first sip of the bubbly. The main course was from Pocklington—a 21-year contract lasting until

1999, the longest in professional sports, which would pay Gretzky around $300,000 per year. On his eighteenth birthday, Wayne Gretzky became a multimillionaire.

"The contract is for personal services," Pocklington told the media. "There's no way anyone's going to touch him when we join the NHL."

If Wayne felt any immediate pressure to live up to his huge contract, he didn't show it one iota. His play was so solid that he was selected to center Gordie Howe and his son Mark in the opener of a three-game series between the WHA all-stars and Moscow Dynamo, an elite Soviet team. He finished his first pro season third in the WHA in scoring with 46 goals and 110 points, and copped the league's Rookie of the Year award.

In the WHA playoffs Wayne led the Oilers to a seven-game semifinal victory over the Hartford Whalers, but fell short in the finals, losing the Avco Cup to the Winnipeg Jets, four games to two. Still, he led all players in playoff scoring with 10 goals and 20 points.

The next time Wayne Gretzky scored a goal, it would be in the National Hockey League.

5

The NHL Phenomenon

WHEN THE NHL AND WHA agreed on a merger in March 1979, four teams, including Edmonton, were absorbed into the established league. (The others were Winnipeg, Quebec, and Hartford.) The Oilers and Winnipeg were placed in the Smythe Division of the Clarence Campbell Conference, which made them part of the league's weakest division. However, besides Gretzky, nineteen-year-old defenseman Kevin Lowe (who would become Wayne's roommate), and nineteen-year-old left wing Mark Messier, the Oilers were a team primarily made up of journeymen veterans. A team like this might be a power in the WHA, but could they cut it in the superior NHL? With the Great Gretzky on our side, Edmonton fans must have thought, anything was possible. And they backed up their belief at the box office, where Oilers fanatics bought almost 15,000 season tickets.

"We've got the guy to build a team around," said Oiler general manager Larry Gordon. "Now we've just got to give him some help."

But the pompous old guard of the NHL wasn't sold. Despite the fact that pro hockey always found it difficult generating media attention—for escapades other than fisticuffs—the league did little to hype its new superstar. Instead, the NHL's muckamucks echoed the same skepticism of Gretzky that he'd heard since his days in Junior hockey. The kid's too small. The kid's too scrawny. The kid won't withstand the tough checking in the NHL. The kid will be lucky to score 20 goals.

The kid again shrugged off the skeptics. "This will be my fifth straight year as a rookie," he announced. "I'm in the NHL at eighteen, just like Bobby Orr and Gordie Howe were. There's gonna be a lot of pressure, but I plan to prove myself. I don't expect to do as well as I did in the other league. I feel I did well for my first year, and now all I can do is my best and hope it's good enough."

At the beginning of the year Wayne played as though he were just feeling his way along, just trying to get his bearings. He didn't dominate games, but he was getting at least a point a day. Opposing teams weren't blatantly running their goons out to intimidate him, but the checking was tight and the slams into the boards were harder than those dished out to less-publicized players.

If anybody did become a tad overzealous in "defending" against Gretzky, by slashing him in the face with a stray stick or hacking on his arms as he crossed the enemy blue line, his bodyguards, including six-foot-three, 215-pound Dave Semenko, a onetime WHA "goon," would protect him. As one coach observed, "Gretzky just kind of rolls his head in the direction of a guy who just hit him, and Semenko moves in." And before one game, Edmonton defenseman Lee Fogolin told tough Detroit Red Wings center Dennis Polonich that "if you touch the kid, you'll have to deal with me."

Seeing how much tough stuff the kid could take was part of Wayne's NHL initiation, and he intuitively understood this particular part of the inner game of hockey.

"I try to stay out of trouble and I'm hard to hit. But when I do get hit, I can take it. I'm not a fighter, but I practice self-defense."

Wayne soon had the entire league practicing defense—against him. By mid-season he was leading the Oilers in scoring by a huge margin, was ranked behind only the Canadiens' Guy Lafleur and the Kings' Marcel Dionne in the league scoring race, and was selected for the All-Star game. Ten days after playing with the league's best, he tied a 33-year old NHL record by assisting on seven goals in a game against the Washington Capitals. It seemed like every night he was putting on a special exhibition for the fans in NHL arenas, fans who either doubted him or just had never seen him flash his bountiful skills.

There was one Oiler home game against the New York Rangers in which Edmonton was trailing 1–0 after two periods. The game appeared lost when Gretzky was carried off the ice on a stretcher after an especially violent hit.

"There didn't seem to be a chance he'd be back in the third period," recalled Ranger goalie John Davidson, "but he comes back and puts on a show. It seemed like he had the puck the entire period. He scores two goals, they win 3–1, and the Edmonton crowd goes nuts. Without him, the Oilers are out of it. With him, they win."

Then there was the March evening he humbled Atlanta Flames' goalie Jim Craig, who was fresh from the triumph of the heroic United States Olympic Team in Lake Placid. The gold-medal victory over the Soviet Union had apparently turned Jim into "Cocky Craig." Atlanta was winning by a couple of goals, and when Gretzky skated through the goal crease in the second period, Craig brazenly snapped, "Hey, Gretzky, just who do you think you are anyway?" Wayne didn't respond —verbally, that is. He responded mentally. Wayne Gretzky was no stereotypical young Canadian "hoser," eh? He remembered watching the Flames practice earlier that day and seeing them work one-on-ones against Craig. He remembered eight skaters going in, cutting to their right and scoring on Craig's stick side. Now he'd put that knowledge to use. With the Oilers down 4–1 in the second period, Wayne received a pass on a breakaway. He skated to his right and lifted the puck over Craig's lazy stick. In the third period he did it again, and scored an additional goal in a 5–4 Oiler victory.

"I didn't think the kid would remember telling me about Craig's stick side," said Sather after the game. "But that's the great thing about him, right? He sees something like that and he files it away. A lot of guys give up, but not this kid. He keeps going at it until the game is over. You can never tell by the way he's playing whether we're down by three or four or ahead by one or two. That's another one of those things that makes him different."

Gretzky put on probably his most impressive show of the season in late March against the Toronto Maple Leafs in front of a Canadian national television audience. *Hockey Night in Canada* is the country's most popular TV show and not even a network executive planning a "sweeps week" could have thought up such an exciting two hours. When viewers weren't watching Gretzky warming up, seeing highlights of his first NHL season, or checking out the home movies Walter Gretzky had taken of his son in the backyard rink, they were watching Gretzky skate the Maple Leafs into submission. Performing his entire repertoire of moves, The Great One scored two goals and had four assists in a stunning 7-5 Edmonton victory.

One goal came on a patented Gretzky move behind the net, which culminated in a backhand goal stuffed behind goalie Mike Palmateer. Another puck was sent into the twine by a quick, sizzling slapshot. But the assists might have been even prettier, and were vintage Gretzky in every way. Skating down the left side of the Leafs' end, he stopped on a dime, then, in a move hockey fans hadn't seen since the heyday of Bobby Orr, he pirouetted 360 degrees before passing to teammate Blair MacDonald for a goal. Later, during an Oiler power play, he held the puck behind the net for what seemed an eternity, then flicked it to an open winger for another score. In the *Hockey Night in Canada* broadcast booth, announcer Gary Dornhoefer said, in the understatement of the year, "You've got to believe in him now." After the game, Toronto coach Joe Crozier moaned, "A lot of people came to watch Gretzky play. So did the Maple Leafs."

But there were occasional downsides to The Great One's dazzling offensive displays. Veteran defenseman Pat Price, a former New York Islander, didn't think it mattered how many goals Gretzky and his linemates were getting if the Oilers weren't winning games. So Price went up to Gretzky one day and said, "Listen, Wayne, you have to start playing better defense."

If Wayne was insulted, he remained cool about it. "Pricey, I'm doing my best to help the team—I can't do it any other way."

Like a savvy coach should, Glen Sather got involved before things could get out of hand. He'd been a tad perturbed at Gretzky's defensive deficiencies in the past, but had learned how to minimize them. In Kevin Lowe's book *Champions*, he related that Sather used "The Stallion Theory" when dealing with Gretzky.

"If you have a stallion that wants to run," Lowe wrote, "you don't rein him in, you want to let him go. Same with Wayne. He had all the natural talent in the world, so let him do what he does best."

Lowe explained that Sather would pull back the reins once in a while and ask Gretzky to play between center ice and Oiler territory instead of hovering at the center red line, where he could get potential breakaways.

"In that way, Sather allowed Gretzky to develop in a manner that a stricter disciplinarian—such as Montreal coach Scotty Bowman—might not have done."

Heading into April, nobody suggested pulling back the reins on the former high school distance runner, who was involved in two important races. One was for the NHL scoring title, in which Gretzky trailed only Dionne by one goal. The other was for the playoffs, and the Oilers were in a desperate sprint to beat out three other teams for the sixteenth and final spot. Would Wayne and the Oilers have a kick left? Does Canada have cold weather? On April 2, Wayne became the youngest player ever to score 50 goals in an NHL season. He was just nineteen years, two months old when his 50th was the Oilers' only goal in a 1-1 contest against Minnesota, the next to last game of the season.

The season finale would be filled with more drama than Wayne had ever experienced in his hockey life. Even if he scored a hat trick and won the scoring title, a loss to the Colorado Rockies would knock the Oilers out of the playoffs. Things looked bleak when the Rockies took an early 2-0 lead. But like a true champion, Wayne showed once again that he was a money player as well as a talented one. He assisted on the tying goal in the second period and produced the game-winning tally in the third. Wayne had given his team a playoff berth. Now he had to find out if 51 goals and 137 points—two points more than Dionne notched—to that point would be enough to give him the Art Ross Trophy as the league's scoring champion.

The Kings were playing in Los Angeles that night, so the results wouldn't be in until early in the morning. While Wayne's teammates were celebrating with him at a restaurant, he excused himself to find out what had happened to Dionne. "When Wayne returned to the table, he had a long face on," recalled Kevin Lowe, "and it was obvious he hadn't won the title." As it turned out, Dionne had tied Gretzky in points, and NHL rules stipulated that in case of a tie, the player with the most goals wins the scoring title. Dionne had outscored Gretzky 53–51.

In the first round of the playoffs, Edmonton lost to the mighty Philadelphia Flyers in three straight games, although two were decided in sudden death. But Wayne had little reason to sulk about the scoring race and the playoffs. Edmonton's day was certainly coming as long as he was around. He could take solace in all the awards and tributes that came pouring in as soon as the '79–80 season ended. Despite losing the scoring title, he was voted the Hart Trophy as the league's Most Valuable Player. He also won the Lady Byng Trophy as the "most gentlemanly player," and was voted the second-team All-Star center behind Dionne.

And a lot of those doubters began eating their words.

"The NHL people were being foolish and very shortsighted," said Minnesota North Star coach Glen Sonmor, who had coached against Gretzky in the WHA. "They hadn't come to appreciate Wayne's gifts, and they underestimated the WHA. And the proof is in what he did as an NHL rookie."

"Smart. That's the first word that comes to mind when I see Gretzky," observed New York Islander coach Al Arbour, who directed his team to the Stanley Cup in 1980. "He knows what he's doing every time he's on the ice."

"There were a couple of games against us," said Philadelphia Flyer captain Bobby Clarke, "where he didn't seem to be doing much. We paid a lot of attention to him any time he was on the ice, but just when we thought we had him figured out, he'd do something he hadn't shown us before, and he'd hurt us. The uncanny thing about his game is the way he can spin and take off. He does that faster and quicker than anybody I've ever seen."

"He has the ability to control the puck and himself," offered Oiler goalie Dave Dryden. "He's able to wait for somebody to make a little mistake, then takes advantage of it for everything it's worth. Most players have preconceived notions of what they're going to do. I'm convinced he doesn't. You can't compare him to anybody else. He's unique."

People found out just how unique Wayne Gretzky was when the Oilers had their players undergo a series of physical tests during the '79–80 season. An eye examination showed that Gretzky had about 30 percent better peripheral vision than anyone else tested. And although he finished last among all the Oilers in sheer physical strength, he showed an almost unnatural ability to recuperate after strenuous activity.

As for Gretzky's on-ice intelligence, writer Peter Gzowski surmised in a 1980 magazine article that it wasn't so much a higher level of thinking that made Wayne such an elite hockey player, but his level of perception which allowed him to attain such excellence.

"What Wayne Gretzky sees on a hockey rink," Gzowski wrote in Canada's *Saturday Night,* "is more simple than what a less accomplished player sees; not so much a set of moving players, as a number of situations—chunks. Standing behind the net in that televised Toronto game, he knew that his wingers would cross. That was a chunk of information. He didn't have to think about it; he could act on it. Passes into what appear to be open spaces on the ice are in reality passes to a place that he knows, not instinctively but through a different level of perception, will be filled by one of his own men."

When Gzowski related his theory to Gretzky, the young hockey genius agreed. "It's all practice, absolutely," he said. "Nine out of ten people think it's instinct, and it isn't."

Whether it was practice, instinct, talent, or genius, it was on display again—and in force—during the 1980–81 season. "If you think Wayne Gretzky is trouble now," Bruin general manager Harry Sinden had observed, "just wait until he's part of a good team." Well, the Oilers were adding some young players with star potential to assist Gretzky in helping Edmonton's climb up the NHL ladder. Young defenseman Kevin Lowe and left wing Mark Messier were already in tow when the Oilers brought on board Paul Coffey, a nineteen-year-old defenseman; twenty-year-old left wing Glenn Anderson; and twenty-year-old Finnish right wing Jari Kurri.

Though Wayne got off to a shaky start due to relentless shadowing by opposing forwards, his game was picking up steam by midseason. Unfortunately, the Oilers' game was not. With just 34 points, they were fifth in the six-team Smythe Division and were looking like anything but a playoff-caliber squad.

"I can pass the puck all night," Gretzky said at one point, obviously frustrated by the team's floundering, "but someone has to put it in the net. One guy can't win or lose the Stanley Cup."

Wayne's teammates appreciated their star's preoccupation with getting them into the flow of the game and setting them up with his crisp, creative passes from behind the net. With three quarters of the season gone, Wayne had scored or assisted on 49 percent of Edmonton's goals. By contrast, when Phil Esposito set the NHL scoring record with 152 points in 1970–71, he was in on only 38 percent of the Boston Bruin goals.

"For me it's just as nice to pass the puck and watch someone else shoot as to score myself," Wayne admitted. To which linemate Blair MacDonald commented, "He's probably the least self-centered superstar you'll ever see. He's a part of the team in every way. His heart is as big as a building."

One prime example of the kind of Gretzky fortitude that inspired his teammates came in a game against the Philadelphia Flyers in late February. The Oilers had never beaten the rambunctious "Broad Street Bullies," and there was pregame talk in the press lounge that Gretzky, as one writer put it, "had a perpetual case of Philadelphia flu." But on this night, after the Oilers fell behind 2–0 in the second period, Wayne made the Flyers ill. In the last 21 minutes he scored two goals, added two assists, and Edmonton romped, 6–2.

"Believe it or not," Glen Sather said after the game, "some hockey people still think of Wayne as a flash in the pan."

The Los Angeles Kings didn't. Before one game against the Oilers, L. A. coach Bob Berry posted a note on the locker room blackboard detailing his team's strategy for Edmonton. The message was simple: stop Gretzky.

"Must be aware of him at all times . . ." the note read. "Likes to shoot against the flow . . . likes to get to blue line and 'buttonhook' defense; force him outside . . . be alert for long pass to him up the middle . . . likes to set up behind our net; try to make him go to his backhand."

"That," revealed Marcel Dionne, "shows what we think of him." By mid-March Gretzky had taken over the scoring lead from Dionne ("I can't get points like he does," said the Kings' star center. "He makes me feel like an old man, and I'm just twenty-nine"), but with only 12 games left in the season, Edmonton was still battling for the 16th and last playoff spot with Washington. Then, suddenly, like an oil well that becomes a gusher, the Oilers erupted. Led by Gretzky, they won 11 out of their last 12 and finished 14th in the league.

In his second NHL season, The Great One was merely fabulous. Down the stretch, he made another assault on the league record book. On March 30 he scored his 153rd and 154th points to break Phil Esposito's single-season point mark. On April 1 his 103rd assist put him past Bobby Orr for the single-season assist record. His five points in the season finale on April 4 gave him 55 goals, a record 109 assists, and a record 164 points, making him the youngest player—twenty years, two months—to win the Art Ross Trophy as the league's scoring champion. And that 164th point had given him 301 for his first two seasons, making him the quickest 300-point scorer ever in NHL history.

"I'd trade my whole team for the kid," raved Maple Leaf owner Harold Ballard, who'd once been one of the nonbelievers, "and I'd throw in the farm club, too."

"I was offered two million for him," revealed Peter Pocklington, "but ten million wouldn't buy him. There's no price on greatness."

The Great Gretzky and the Oilers were on a roll that carried them to an unbelievable three-game upset sweep of the mighty Montreal Canadiens, a team that had won four of the last five Stanley Cups and had finished third in the league in 1980–81. In Game One, Wayne tied a Stanley Cup playoff record with five assists (he also scored a goal) in a 6–3 win. And in the Oilers' subsequent 3–1 and 6–2 victories, he scored two goals and had three more assists. He had 11 points, while Montreal's great Guy Lafleur (who Wayne regarded with enormous respect) had just one. When Wayne was on the ice during even-strength situations, Edmonton outscored Montreal 11–0. The superstar torch was being passed to The Great One by yet another NHL legend.

In his unrestrained joy at beating the Canadiens, Wayne was quoted saying some things he would eventually regret. In the first flush of victory, he said, "The thing that hit me first was, 'Geez, we beat the Montreal Canadiens.' We beat the best organization in the history of hockey. I guess that's something, isn't it?" Then days later, talking to the New York media, which seizes on story angles like tigers go after raw meat, he remarked, "We had to be prepared mentally and physically to beat the best team in hockey."

Such pronouncements are the stuff of opposition locker-room walls. And naturally, the New York Islanders, defending Stanley Cup champions, didn't take kindly to the scoring champion's remarks. The Isles hardly needed any prodding, but the Big Apple media, as they are wont to do, added fuel to the fire.

"For all his precocious genius on the ice," wrote *New York Times* columnist Dave Anderson, "Wayne Gretzky is indisputably twenty years old in coping with the psychology of playoff diplomacy. By complimenting the Canadiens, he unthinkingly had insulted the Islanders." The *New York Post* chipped in with the headline: ISLES WANT TO MAKE GRETZKY EAT HIS WORDS.

Actually, they stuffed them down his throat. The first two games were 8–2 and 6–3 Islander romps. But it was a tribute to Gretzky that with the media controversy swirling around him, he came up with a three-goal hat trick in a 5–2 Oiler victory in Game Three. "It was a thing of beauty, Hall of Fame stuff," wrote Jim Matheson in the *Edmonton Journal.* "He put on the kind of moves that the NHL's greatest legends would have applauded in that great league in the sky."

"With a player of Wayne's skills," said Al Arbour after the game, "you just hope to contain him. But a player that great can't be contained forever, so you just say, okay, he got hot. Now let's get on with the next game."

After Edmonton lost a tough 5–4 game in overtime, they came back in Game Five with a 4–3 win, but the Islanders' experience was just too much for the young, exuberant Oilers. In front of their home fans they succumbed in Game Six, 5–2. The Islanders then went on to win their second straight Stanley Cup.

"The Islanders showed us we're not ready to win right now," Gretzky said after the playoffs, in which he totaled seven goals and 21 points in nine games. "The most important thing we did was create a winning attitude. We matured tremendously, maybe even a year or so, in a span of a couple of weeks. We know what it takes to be a winner, and we know how much work it will take to go even further. We showed ourselves and, I think, the rest of hockey, that the Oilers are a team to be watched. I think we're on our way."

If Wayne experienced any disappointment after the playoff defeat, it was eased somewhat when he found he'd been voted his second straight Hart Trophy as the NHL's Most Valuable Player and was named the league's first team All-Star center. What could Wayne Gretzky possibly do for an encore now? St. Louis Blues' coach Red Berenson probably echoed the thoughts of the rest of the league when he said, "He's only twenty, and he's torn the NHL apart two years a row. It's scary to think what he might do before he's done."

6

The Babe Ruth of Hockey

In 1919 BASEBALL'S BOSTON RED SOX converted a terrific left-handed pitcher named Babe Ruth into a pitcher/outfielder, and the powerful man responded by hitting a record 29 home runs, five more than the previous mark, set in 1915. Ruth was sold to the New York Yankees the following season and promptly transformed baseball from a singles-hitter's game to a slugger's paradise. As an everyday rightfielder playing in the Polo Grounds in 1920 and 1921, Ruth walloped 54 and 59 homers, respectively (over 30 more than his immediate challenger for the home run crown), and drove in 308 runs over the two seasons.

Playing in Yankee Stadium (known as

"The House that Ruth Built") in 1927, the "Bambino" smashed his own record by smacking 60 homers, 13 more than teammate Lou Gehrig. In rewriting the record books, Ruth had also redefined baseball. There was The Babe and everybody else, and he became the most famous and beloved sports hero in America.

It wasn't quite The Great One and everybody else prior to the 1981–82 hockey season, but if Wayne Gretzky wasn't yet the Babe Ruth of hockey, he was coming awfully close. He had already shattered the NHL records for assists and points, the baseball equivalent to runs batted in and runs scored. Still out there for the twenty-year-old to grab was hockey's home run title—goals scored. Phil Esposito had set the record in 1971–72, when he scored 76 in 78 games (breaking Bobby Hull's 1968–69 total of 58 in 76 contests). If The Great Gretzky could average a point a game the previous season, couldn't he average a goal a game—which would give him 80—with a year more experience and a better supporting cast? Could the bulbous Babe Ruth eat hot dogs and drink beer?

But there were other questions to answer before the '81–82 season would begin. The first one was: Could a Gretzky-led Team Canada win the Canada Cup in September against the best hockey teams in the world?

The pre-NHL-season exhibition would include national teams from the Soviet Union, Sweden, Finland, Czechoslovakia, and the United States. Team Canada's squad was made up entirely of NHL All-Stars, and Gretzky realized one of his dreams when he was chosen to center a line including the Canadiens' exciting superstar Guy Lafleur, who was known as "The Flower."

"To play on a line with Lafleur, even if it's just training camp, is an enormous thrill for me," Wayne admitted. "I've been like everyone else for the past years; I've been in awe of the things Guy has done in hockey rinks."

It didn't take long for Gretzky to establish himself as one of the greatest players in the world. He scored two goals and had an assist in the second period of Team Canada's 9–0 trouncing of Finland. In the second game, against the United States, Gretzky assisted on a first-period Lafleur goal, then scored one himself in the second. With the score tied 3–3 in the third, he assisted on a power-play goal scored by the Islanders' Mike Bossy, and later notched another talley. Team Canada won their second game of the series 8–3.

Wayne was shut down during the 4–4 tie against the Czechs, but he was *knocked* down —often—during a controversial 4–3 victory against Sweden. The Swedes may be famous for their pacifist nature off the ice, but during this particular encounter they were as aggressive and chippy as a nasty NHL squad. As the

Czechs had done in silencing Gretzky, the Swedes shadowed him, roughed him up, kept him off balance. But they also took it a step further. They used their sticks as weapons of intimidation. As Montreal defenseman Larry Robinson observed, "When the Swedes decide they want to play physical, their sticks come up. They just don't have the knack of playing tough without the other stuff."

At first Gretzky was knocked to ice by a brutal check, and Gilbert Perreault of the Buffalo Sabres broke his right ankle trying to avoid a collision with his fallen teammate. Then later, Lars Lindgren, a Vancouver Canuck defenseman playing for his native land during the series, slashed Gretzky across the left arm as Wayne skated through the Swedish defensive zone. Skin was broken in Gretzky's elbow area, he sustained a severe bruise, and the muscles began to spasm. The pain was so intense, he couldn't take face-offs in the third period.

"Are these Swedes goons or what?" Gretzky asked with a touch of anger after the game. Then he added, "But I won't retaliate. I don't work that way. The best retaliation when someone gives you a cheap shot is to go around him and score."

And that's exactly what he did just 58 seconds into the next match against the mighty Soviet Union. Though he complained of a sore left arm and elbow, he also set up

Lafleur and notched another assist in a 7–3 victory. When Team Canada beat the U.S. 4–1, while the Soviets defeated the Czechs by the same score, it set up a final showdown between the two best teams in the world. "If we win," said Wayne, who had gradually become the team spokesman despite his youth, "then everything will be okay because the Canadian fans expect us to win. But if we lose, we're really going to hear about it."

Gretzky was teamed with Marcel Dionne and Lafleur in the final, but not even this superstar threesome could fathom the superb Soviet style. Ahead 3–1 going into the third period, the Russians scored within the first two minutes of the final stanza, and Team Canada immediately collapsed, ultimately losing 8–1. The Great One couldn't save his countrymen, and as Wayne predicted, they heard about it. The next issue of the weekly hockey bible, *The Hockey News*, said it all by wailing, WOE CANADA! across its front page.

With a new NHL season approaching, Canadian hockey fans couldn't mourn Team Canada's defeat for long. Optimism was especially high in Edmonton, which boasted a team with maturing young stars, a new goalie in nineteen-year-old Grant Fuhr (who had been the Oilers' first pick in the June 1981 draft and became the NHL's first black goaltender), and, of course, their twenty-year-old superstar, who was determined to assault the record books with even more of a vengeance this season.

One record on Wayne's mind was the one that had gotten Mike Bossy so much publicity the previous season. When Bossy scored twice against the Quebec Nordiques on January 24, 1981, he became the first player since the legendary Maurice Richard in 1945 to score 50 goals in 50 games. Certainly that was a mark a goal-scoring machine like Wayne Gretzky could achieve. But when Wayne started the season "on fire," as New York Ranger announcer Marv Albert might have said, people began to wonder whether Gretzky could score 50 goals in *40* games.

Wouldn't that be impossible, even for The Great One? It seemed that way when he scored "just" seven goals in his first 11 games. Then in late October, Gretzky scored 17 goals in 14 games, and went on another tear in early December, scoring 12 goals in six games, including four in game 38 against the Los Angeles Kings. All he needed to reach another incredible milestone was five goals in his next two games. On the afternoon of game 39 against the tough-checking Philadelphia Flyers, Wayne turned to teammate Kevin Lowe and boldly said, "I think I can do it tonight." That would mean he would have to score five goals, something accomplished only 17 times since 1930.

But Gretzky was saying something quite

different for press consumption. Just before the game he told the assembled media that "against a tough team like Philadelphia the chances don't come as often. And as anyone approaches a record, it always seems more difficult to score. It wouldn't surprise me if the next five goals are the toughest of my career, because nobody wants to be the victim of a record and I'll be checked very closely."

It almost seemed as though Wayne was purposely setting up the ultimate challenge for himself. He wouldn't be getting any extra money for scoring 50 goals in 40 games or less. The Oilers, who were developing into a dominant team by this point, wouldn't get any extra points in the standings. And even if he'd been shut out for two games, Gretzky would still hit the 50-goal plateau faster than anybody in NHL history. But in Wayne's mind the record became 50 goals in 40 games, and he was determined to break this fantasy mark.

"Wayne has simply got to be the first," observed veteran Oiler defenseman Leo Fogolin in *Sports Illustrated.* "With him there's no other way. If someone takes the puck from him, he starts to get red spots on his face and he becomes very intent. Next time out he'll go like the wind, lift the tempo up a notch. And he'll keep lifting it until he's gotten even."

Just how intense Wayne could be was immediately obvious to Flyer captain Bobby

Clarke during the game. "Gretzky was playing like a man obsessed," said Clarke. "He just kept materializing out of nowhere." Wayne emerged in front of the Flyer goal to put a Paul Coffey rebound home for goal number 46 at 7:47 of the first period. Then, a little over two minutes later, he sent a 20-foot slapshot under the right crossbar. In the second period a 25-foot slapshot whistled over goalie Pete Peeters's right shoulder. The 17,490 Oiler fans who packed the Coliseum hoping to see history in the making were in a frenzy. Gretzky now had a hat trick, 48 goals, and over a period and a half to try for two more.

The Flyers managed to shut Wayne down until five minutes into the third period, when goal 49 came on another 20-foot drive after he had intercepted a pass. "The place got as loud as any arena I'd ever been in," said Clarke, who had played on a Stanley Cup champion. The score was now Edmonton 6, Philadelphia, 3. "We wanted to win the game, sure, but we were all thinking about feeding Wayne," said Oiler defenseman Paul Coffey. "That was it. Get the puck to Wayne, get him to 50, and we'll win anyway."

The Flyers staged a valiant comeback, and with 74 seconds left Coach Pat Quinn removed Pete Peeters. Gretzky would now have an empty net to shoot at. After Oiler goalie Grant Fuhr blocked a shot that landed on the stick of Glenn Anderson, the winger, who instinctively knew Gretzky would be around center ice, sent a pass in that direction. Wayne grabbed the puck, skated in on one Philly defender and launched a 45-foot shot that found the open net. Oiler fans went crazy as the Flyers looked on in complete awe.

"What he is doing is obscene," said Bobby Clarke. "There are going to be records broken, but not the way he is doing it. You hear, well, the game has changed, it's more wide-open since expansion. Then why hasn't anyone else done what Gretzky is doing? I'll tell you why—because he's *that* much better than the rest of us."

"He's made the record book obsolete," said Minnesota North Stars GM Lou Nanne about The Great One. "From now on, Gretzky's only point of reference is himself."

If Gretzky were merely considered a phenomenon before breaking the 50-50 record, he was now clearly a living legend. And for the publicity-starved NHL, he was a savior who was filling hockey rinks in cities that rarely had sellouts, earning astronomical ticket prices for scalpers, and bringing in busloads of media. In Pittsburgh, a Saturday night game that usually attracted 13,000 fans generated 16,000 when Edmonton came to town. In Toronto, which regularly sold out, scalpers reportedly were getting $200 to $800 for a pair of tickets to the Leafs-Oilers game. In Buffalo the Sabres had to accommodate two hundred media people instead of the usual seventy. And during Edmonton's January East Coast road trip, there were 132 Gretzky interview requests.

Though most fans wanted to know what all the fuss was about with this guy Gretzky, The Great One was hardly a one-man show, even though Coach Sather was giving him abnormally long two-minute shifts, playing him 32 to 38 minutes a game and moving him from line to line. "I'm like a guy showing off a precious gem in different pawnshops," said Sather in explaining his strategy. By mid-January the Oilers had won 28, lost nine and tied seven, and Wayne was on an astounding 221-point pace for the season. But if Gretzky was the Babe Ruth of hockey, the Edmonton kids were becoming the sport's "Murderers' Row," the monicker of the 1927 New York Yankees baseball team. Five Oilers besides Gretzky were on a pace to score more than 30 goals, and most credited Wayne—who had set up 14 different teammates for goals by February—with their inflated statistics.

"Playing with Wayne's a career break," admitted Jari Kurri. "With him, you know your goals and assists will go up." Dave Lumley, who was a twenty-seven-year-old journeyman forward "thinking about getting a job driving a truck," was added to Gretzky's line when some injuries hit, and was instantly transformed from an ugly duckling into a scoring swan. He notched goals in 12 straight games—one short of an NHL record—and produced 20 goals in 20 games overall. "Wayne's like having your own Fantasy Island," said Lumley ("Goals, boss, goals!"). "It's so much fun to play with him. I had no goals and no assists before getting on his line, and then I almost made the record books."

Even the league's goaltenders, whom Wayne was embarrassing nightly, were filled with praise for their number-one nemesis. After two seasons of watching Gretzky gyrations with the puck, they had no choice but to put him on a par with the game's best shooters. He didn't have the thundering slap-shot of Lafleur or the lightning release of Mike Bossy, but goals rained down around him, nonetheless.

"He has an extraordinary knack for catching the goalie off guard," observed St. Louis Blues' goalie Mike Liut.

"Wayne's shot is not that hard, but it's deceptive," added Hartford goalie John Garrett. "The first time it'll come at you pretty fast. The next time he'll use the same motion but take something off the shot. He'll wind up for the full slapshot, then send the puck at you like a knuckleball. And he's accurate. His shot is on the corner all the time."

Another veteran netminder marveled at Gretzky's coordination of his skating and shooting. "He makes a goalie nervous because of his great timing," the goalie said. "He gets the puck and waits, and waits—and waits. If you budge the least bit in the nets, he lets it go and finds an opening."

Greg Millen of the Pittsburgh Penguins admired The Great One's ice intelligence. "He's the smartest shooter in the league," Millen remarked. "He beats you with his brains. When he skates toward the goalie, then cuts to his left, the goalie instinctively moves left, too. Then Wayne puts the puck in the right corner."

Opposition coaches soon became obsessed with stopping this young dynamo on skates. Everyone had a theory on how to do it. One coach felt it best to assign one defensive-oriented center to shadow Gretzky for the entire game. Whenever Wayne was on the ice, that particular center would come on to check him. Of course, that poor center would probably be a basket-case by the game's end, what with the extensive amount of ice time Gretzky was being given by Glen Sather. Another team tried to have its defensemen constantly converge on Gretzky, but with Wayne's superior vision on the ice and great passing skills, he was merely able to set up his forwards more easily. The Montreal Canadiens had a bit more success in stopping the whirlwind. They would vigorously forecheck Gretzky's wingers and assign a couple of centers (whoever's line was on the ice) to stay on top of Gretzky.

Toronto Maple Leaf coach Mike Nykoluk believed the best strategy was to treat Gretzky like any other center, to check him tightly but not to the exclusion of defending against the other four men on the ice. "Assigning just one player to do nothing but cover Gretzky detracts from the game," Nykoluk pointed out. "Hockey is a team sport, and that's the only way to play it. If you put one guy on Gretzky, that guy will run into penalties—holding, interference, tripping. You can't relieve the rest of your players of the responsibility. Besides, you'd also be telling them that they couldn't do the job, and that's no good, either.

"Gretzky passes so well that crowding him is dangerous," Nykoluk added. "So it's got to be a five-man chore. He's going to have the odd good shift no matter what. He's that great. But I can live with that as long as there's been an honest effort against him."

But despite all the praise and all the opposition hair-pulling Gretzky was causing, there were just some people—as there had been his whole, young hockey life—Wayne Gretzky couldn't please. For every dozen supporters, there seemed to be a detractor. After being named a unanimous first-team All-Star in February, one New York hockey writer called Wayne "The Not So Great Gretzky" and lambasted him for lackluster defensive play.

"With Gretzky leading Mike Bossy by 38 points," wrote Mark Everson of *The New York Post,* "there's no way he should be third in the league in plus-minus (the difference between goals scored and goals against while a player is on the ice) if he's working his own zone at all." Everson pointed out that Gretzky was on the ice for 98 even-strength goals for and 62 even-strength goals against, for a 3–2 ratio, while Mike Bossy and Brian Trottier of the Islanders had ratios around 2–1.

"He's never in the defensive zone," criticized former coach Fred Shero in the Everson article. "When the puck goes in, you lose sight of him for five seconds. His wingers and defensemen have to do all the work for him while he makes all the money. Pretty soon they're going to get a little resentful about that."

If Gretzky's Oiler teammates were becoming resentful, it wasn't obvious. After all, this was their meal ticket, the guy who was going to bring them the Stanley Cup. "Everybody knows that he's lacking defensively," said one defenseman who'd played with Wayne in the WHA. "But the best defense is a good offense, and most of the time, he has the puck."

It wasn't Gretzky's defense that people cared much about during February because The Great One was zeroing in on Phil Esposito's single-season scoring record. All the talk wasn't so much about *if* Wayne would do it, but in how many games. Espo had scored his 76 during a 78-game season. Gretzky would probably smash the record in a little over 60 games, and at the rate he was going, he might have a chance for an amazing 90 goals.

Wayne was up to 75 when the Oilers went into Detroit to play their 63rd game of the season. With 20,270 Red Wings fans in attendance, Gretzky tantalizingly collected four assists as Edmonton went up 6–3. With a little over three minutes left in the game, Glenn Anderson sent a pass to Gretzky waiting in the slot and Wayne banged it past goalie Bob Sauve. Espo's record was now tied and the Detroit fans roared their approval.

"I said before I left Edmonton," said Gretzky after the game, "that Detroit was my team when I was a kid, and it's an honor for me to tie the record here."

Some people suggested to Esposito, who was attending all the Oiler games as Gretzky assaulted his record, that the NHL wasn't nearly as good as it was 11 years earlier, when Phil had scored his 76.

"That's a lot of crap," roared the always opinionated Esposito. "Players are bigger and better and shoot harder today. Gretzky has more talent than anyone I've seen since Bobby Orr. He has the ability to concentrate, which few players have."

Three days later, on February 24 in Buffalo, Gretzky was the epitome of cool. "I think I'm going to get one more goal this season," he said. "I don't see any reason to get uptight about it."

In the first period of the Sabres game, Wayne's only shot was stopped by Buffalo goalie Donnie Edwards, but the Oilers managed a 3–1 lead anyway. Edwards stopped three more Gretzky blasts in the second and kept his team in the game long enough for them to tie it. "We started getting caught up in the record goal and not playing our game," said Glen Sather later. "Poor Wayne, everybody on the ice was either trying to feed him or guard him. It was getting too sloppy."

Early in the third period Gretzky appeared to have the historic goal, but Edwards, who was reading Wayne's every move on this particular night, made a diving glove save. With under seven minutes to go in the game, Sabre right wing Steve Patrick fumbled the puck near his own blue line and Gretzky seized the moment. He grabbed the disk, dodged Patrick, and skated toward the net. As Wayne moved in on Edwards, he was hooked by a desperate Buffalo defenseman but still managed to snap a wrist shot under Edwards's arm. Esposito leaped from his seat, raised a fist in the air and yelled "all right." But before Espo and the rest of the fans could compose themselves, Gretzky scored two more goals in the last 1:44 to finish the night with a record 79.

In the joyous locker room Gretzky read a congratulatory telegram from President Ronald Reagan and accepted kudos from Esposito, who told him, "When you got it, I felt goose bumps, I was so excited."

Gretzky continued to create excitement in the hockey world by scoring another 13 goals over the Oilers' final 16 games. All told, he ended the season with an incomprehensible 92 goals, 120 assists, 212 points, and ten hat tricks, all NHL records. To illustrate just how dominant Wayne was, consider that the league's number-two scorer, Mike Bossy, notched 64 goals and 147 points.

Unfortunately for Wayne and the Oilers, the heady days of February and March turned into the dog days of April. Edmonton had registered the NHL's second-best record (111 points to the Islanders' 118), and in the first round of the Stanley Cup playoffs faced a Los Angeles Kings team that was 17 games under .500. But the Oilers, who coasted through the end of the regular schedule, played sloppily throughout the best-of-five series. And despite their poor record, the Kings still boasted a potent offense led by Marcel Dionne, Dave Taylor, and Charlie Simmer, three sharpshooters who would be facing the talented yet inexperienced Grant Fuhr in the Edmonton goal.

Had Gretzky not scored a sudden-death

goal in Game Two, the Oilers might have been ousted in three straight. As it was, the Kings battled Edmonton to a fifth game, and as every sports fan knows, anything can happen in a final game. To Gretzky and the Oilers, it was the worst that could happen. The Kings won 7–4 to produce one of Cup history's greatest upsets. In Edmonton sports writers were calling it the biggest "choke" in Stanley Cup history and they were calling the Oilers "weak-kneed wimps."

Wayne was as disappointed and as drained as he'd ever been in his hockey life. If he could have only traded one record for one victory against the Kings . . . Personal records are great, but how many opportunities are there to win the Stanley Cup?

"We're going to have to learn from our mistakes," he said after scoring a goal in the final game. "We took two steps forward beating Montreal and extending the Islanders last year, and now we've gone backwards. Well, we're going to have to take another huge step forward next year. It takes a big man to face his mistakes, but it takes a bigger man to correct his mistakes. We can't get down because of it. We just have to do what it takes to go all the way the next time."

Though it was little consolation, Wayne still had his new records and awards to be proud of over the long summer off-season. Besides winning the Art Ross Trophy as the leading scorer for the second straight year, Wayne also was easily voted his third successive Hart Trophy as Most Valuable Player. Even more special was being named the recipient of the Lester B. Pearson award, emblematic of the league's outstanding player as selected by the players.

It was a "Ruthian" season by any standard, one that was sure to bring Wayne Gretzky more accolades, more endorsement deals, more money and fame. And at the ripe old age of twenty-one, The Great One was becoming Wayne Gretzky, Inc., the NHL's best salesman and the sports world's hottest property.

7

The Hot Commodity

IN THE FASCINATING, fickle, and increasingly financial world of sports, a professional athlete usually doesn't become a money-making machine—for himself, his agent, his team owner, and companies selling commercial products—until he leads his team to a championship and can shout "I'm going to Disney World" to a national television audience. Such is the profile of our new national heroes. But by the summer of 1982, Wayne Gretzky was such a phenomenon people wanted to throw money at him. They wanted to capitalize on his name even though his team hadn't won a Stanley Cup and NHL games were not being seen on an American television network.

In Canada the selling of Wayne Gretzky

had already begun by the summer of 1980. Besides lending his name to a variety of hockey-equipment manufacturers, Gretzky was filming commercials for a jeans company, 7-Up soft drinks (in a spot which also featured his younger brother Keith, who is now a 22-year-old center for the minor league affiliate of the Buffalo Sabres), and a chocolate bar for a Canadian candy company. During the shooting of the candy-bar spot, Wayne proved he had as much panache in front of the camera as on the ice. "I guess this is the first time a contract actually melted away," he quipped. "I can really sink my teeth into this . . . You could say it's the sweetest deal I ever signed."

Literally speaking, the sweetest deal Gretzky signed at that time was the one he autographed during the 1981–82 season. Earlier in the year his agent, Gus Badali, and Oiler owner Peter Pocklington had begun dickering over a new contract, and by January they had agreed upon a deal that would pay Gretzky approximately $1 million per year.

Wayne's well-publicized salary, coupled with his record-breaking season, only served to make him an even hotter commodity. There were so many offers, Badali added a business/marketing manager named Michael Barnett to Gretzky's off-ice team. The threesome soon had Wayne's name linked with a life insurance company, a men's cologne, a sportswear company, a video game, a doll, wallpaper, and lunch boxes. Together, Wayne's endorsements were bringing in about $2 million. At the same time there were negotiations with a major automobile manufacturer that had never used a celebrity athlete to hawk its product, and a cereal company was spending $100,000 to develop a Wayne Gretzky breakfast food. The bigger companies had no doubt heard about what a business marriage with Gretzky had done for Titan hockey sticks. The company's sales had rocketed from 13th place to first in the industry right after The Great One began endorsing them.

Some people wondered if Wayne was being spread too thin, if things were getting out of his control. Although he insisted on having the final say about all proposed deals, Wayne admitted to one writer that some things were screened and rejected by his agents.

"Sometimes I feel like Gus and Michael rush some things by me," he told the *Edmonton Journal*'s Terry Jones. "But that's what I hire them to do. I don't have time to worry about all those things that come as a result of what happens on the ice. My number-one priority has to be playing hockey."

Among those things the Badali/Barnett team rejected was a sporting-goods company that wanted to put Wayne's name on a baseball glove. Barnett turned them down because, as he told *People* magazine, "we're not a take-the-money-and-run organization." They also wouldn't cut deals with cigarette or alcohol companies, which was in keeping with Badali's strategy to "project an image of a guy who cares about people, whom success hasn't changed."

The Gretzky image was carefully fashioned through the media, which treated the kid as the new darling of sports. Prior to the 1982–83 season, he had already been on the cover of *Sports Illustrated* and had been featured in *People, Time,* and *Newsweek.* Every publication not only chronicled Gretzky's fabulous ice feats, but his love for soap operas, baseball, steak and potatoes, pizza, tea, and junk food. "I play best on four hot dogs with mustard and onions," he revealed in one publication. "People ask me what's my secret on ice? Bad breath."

Gretzky had been used to the give and take with the media since his Junior hockey days and was extremely comfortable in front of cameras and microphones. He also seemed to instinctively know the proper thing to say, a talent that earned him very favorable press throughout the world. When he returned from a trip to the Soviet Union in August of '82, where he made a film with Russian goalie Vladislav Tretiak, he told the *Toronto Star,* "The thing that made me feel at home was being interviewed by newspapers, radio, and television."

Just three seasons after he was a seventeen-year old phenom in the WHA (left, in 1978–79), Gretzky broke Phil Esposito's single-season goal-scoring record when he put in his 77th against the Buffalo Sabres (below). Wayne finished the 1981–82 season with an amazing 92 goals, which is still the league record. (Photos by Bruce Bennett)

The Great Gretzky consoles Espo after breaking his record. (Bruce Bennett)

Gretzky's great sense of anticipation, superior peripheral vision, and deceptive skating skills have always made him a constant threat on the ice. (Bruce Bennett)

(Photos by Bruce Bennett)

Even when the opposition strategy is to double-team or body check Gretzky, The Great One still seems to create scoring opportunities at will.

Wayne scored 13 goals in the 1983–84 playoffs, leading Edmonton to its first Stanley Cup and ending the four-year reign of the New York Islanders. And, of course, the first is always the sweetest. (Bruce Bennett)

The Oilers' captain hoisted the Stanley Cup for the second straight year in 1985 and set a record for most points (47) in a playoff year. (Bruce Bennett)

Wayne has always been extremely close to his family. His father Walter (above) started teaching him the game of hockey when he was two. At right, the youngest of his three brothers, Brent, helps Wayne celebrate the 1985 Stanley Cup win.

The two-time Stanley Cup Champion Oilers placed nine players on the 1985–86 Campbell Conference All-Star squad, including Gretzky (above, second from left). Wayne, who holds the All-Star record for most goals in one game (four in 1983) has been a first- or second-team All-Star every year he's been in the NHL. (Bruce Bennett)

The trophies Wayne has won since he was a peewee player could fill a house. As of 1989, The Great Gretzky has copped the Hart Trophy (held by Gretzky) as the NHL's Most Valuable Player nine times in ten years. He's won the Art Ross, as the league's scoring leader, seven times. (Bruce Bennett)

Wayne and the Oilers collected a lot of hardware after the 1984–85 season, including their second Stanley Cup (second from left). Gretzky won the Ross and Hart trophies that year, while teammate Paul Coffey won the Norris Trophy as the NHL's best defenseman. (Bruce Bennett)

Two months after Wayne and the Oilers won their fourth Stanley
Cup in 1988 (above), Gretzky married actress Janet Jones.

The Great One cried at the August 1988 press conference announcing the trade that shook Canada...

...but was smiling a few days later when he had his coming-out party as a member of the Los Angeles Kings.

(Photos by Bruce Bennett)

The Great One, who hopes to skate Los Angeles to its first Stanley Cup in 1990, scored 54 goals in his first season as a King and helped defeat his former Oilers teammates in the '89 playoffs.

With an abundance of stories being written about athletes succumbing to the evils of drugs, the down-to-earth image projected of Gretzky through the media must have been a welcome relief to the parents of children who worshiped the kid from Ontario. Take a *People* article, for example, that revealed that Wayne had never bought himself a car, but that of the seven cars owner Peter Pocklington had given him, he had turned over six to members of his family. Then the article quoted Wayne as saying, "I enjoy the money to buy things when I need to. Money can distract and corrupt, it's true. But I was taught priorities by my parents, and I don't worry."

During the '81–82 season Wayne visited the Edmonton Children's Hospital, and in the midst of fawning kids and giggling nurses, one disbelieving boy took a look at the hockey player's quite average physique and said, "No way you're Wayne Gretzky. I can't believe you're the one who's got all those goals."

"I know what you mean," said Gretzky. "Sometimes I can't believe it, either."

Who couldn't be completely charmed by this proud, patient, modest, unspoiled, self-possessed, mature, blue-eyed blond kid who loved his parents and had turned his craft into an art form?

Certainly not the media and the companies and organizations that were trying to capitalize on Gretzky's fame so fast and furiously that many people wondered if Wayne were being pushed too hard. Oiler management urged Gretzky to take at least a month off before and after the season to, as Pocklington put it, "get his head back together and his body to rest after eight months of torture."

During one of these self-imposed vacations, Wayne went to Martinique (in the West Indies), where he hoped nobody would recognize him. While lazing around the beach one day, he saw a man shooting a ball at a paper cup with a Wayne Gretzky Titan hockey stick. "The guy turned out to be from France," he said. "I couldn't believe it."

Wayne never really seemed to tire of being in the limelight. After all, what red-blooded, twenty-one-year-old star athlete would? "I'm not a private person," he told *People* magazine. "I like the attention. The only thing is, every person is human and normal, but sometimes I can't be. I can't stand in the street and holler at someone and get mad. Sometimes I get that urge, but I can't let it out. It's just part of being in sports."

Nobody would have been surprised if success had changed Wayne Gretzky, especially considering the almost godlike aura he was developing in Canada. Barnett called it "a level of hysteria which has ceased to make him an athlete star, but turned him into a pop star." During his amazing '81–82 season, Wayne's fan mail was up to 20,000 pieces a week and had to be delivered in garbage bags to the Northlands Coliseum. Almost every letter contained a request for an autographed picture, and Wayne actually spent a few hours every couple of days signing the photos as a form of relaxation.

In Edmonton his face was more ubiquitous than Alberta oil wells. His mug was plastered on jigsaw puzzles, T-shirts, key chains, billboards, and drugstore counters. It was hard to find a kid who wasn't wearing a number 99 jersey to the hockey games, and every teenage girl wanted to marry him. Said one hockey writer: "They should rename the place Gretmonton."

The city fathers, in fact, were ready to name Wayne their unofficial king. The Great One was doing more to create a sense of civic pride than any gimmick a chamber of commerce could mastermind. One government official said Gretzky had more charisma than the whole Edmonton Eskimos team in the Canadian Football League.

"He has done more to put Edmonton on the map than any other individual or event that I know of," pronounced the official. "I can't think of anything, other than the discovery of oil in 1947, that has been so positive for Edmonton."

The Gretzky phenomenon should have been just as vital for the National Hockey League, but the NHL was never known for organizational brilliance or incisive marketing judgments. When it came to promoting their sport, the league was always its own worst enemy. One example of this occurred during the '81–82 season, when Wayne was invited to be a guest on Johnny Carson's *Tonight Show*. Wayne had been traveling with the Oilers on the road and realized that the only way he'd be able to make the appearance was to rent a jet for $6000. Expecting only $1000 for his appearance on the Carson show, he suggested that the NHL pick up half the rental fee. The league said no, and a golden opportunity to promote Gretzky and hockey through a national television audience was blown like a player missing an empty-net scoring chance.

When he wasn't endorsing products, signing autographs in shopping centers, making friends with celebrities like Alan Thicke (a fellow Canadian who would eventually star in the popular TV show *Growing Pains)*, and appearing on television shows, Wayne was getting involved in a multitude of charitable causes (many of which he is still connected with). Early in his career he worked with the Heart Foundation, the United Way, the Red Cross, and was honorary chairman of the Non-Smokers League. He sponsored golf tournaments for Canada's mentally retarded and tennis tourneys for the Canadian Institute for the Blind. In fact, Wayne donated so much to charities, he won a humanitarian award when he was nineteen. And by 1987 he was giving $300,000 annually to about 65 percent of the recognized charity organizations in Canada.

Also by '87, Gretzky had led his team to a couple of Stanley Cup championships, won a few more MVP awards, and was becoming a one-man conglomerate, a young man who would be set for life if he never earned another dollar from hockey. Gus Badali was out as Wayne's agent, and Michael Barnett, who was now president of an outfit he started with Gretzky called CorpSport International, was running the show with some help from Walter Gretzky. One of the first things they did was to renegotiate a new five-year contract with Pocklington that would pay Wayne an annual salary of nearly $1.5 million a year.

"We look for blue-chip endorsements of a long-term nature," Barnett explained to the *Edmonton Sun.* "Most U.S. companies want you for one message, until the next hot or off-the-wall act comes along. We want to be associated with companies that have the same reputation in their field as Wayne has in his. We want arrangements that will carry on long after Wayne's playing days are over. Money is seldom the determining factor."

CorpSport was generating so many endorsements and so much money for Gretzky, they signed on a business manager named Ian Barrigan to help handle Wayne's financial affairs—which included stock in various companies, and treasury bills, investments in real estate, ownership of a Quebec Junior hockey-league franchise—and to screen the three or four proposals a day that were coming into CorpSport.

"I know it's a cliché, but he's better off the ice than on," said Barrigan about his most famous client. "He's just a tremendous individual, a person you can look up to. He could pick up the phone and get through to anyone he wanted to talk to. That's how much pull the man has."

How did such a young man, a man who never went to college and had spent most of his life on ice hockey rinks, become such a natural salesman, spokesman, and businessman? Was it all an act? Was it the greatest selling job in all of sports by people who knew how to pull the right strings? Was the magic all an illusion?

"The magic is real," claimed Barnett in the *Edmonton Sun* in 1987. "Saying Wayne is being 'sold' is a bad choice of words. He's just had a good perception of life and values since a young age. His father built a foundation and Wayne took it from there. Believe me, it's real. There have been times when I've learned about marketing from Wayne. There are experts in public relations who would do themselves a favor if they learned from him."

Gretzky's name and likeness are now as-

sociated with, among other things, a General
Mills cereal called ProStars, Traveller's Insurance, Lloyd's Bank of Canada, Gillette Canada,
Nissan (with whom he signed a six-year deal
in '87), Canon cameras (which plastered
Gretzky's face on a huge billboard in New
York's Times Square in 1985), and Nike (in
1989 Gretzky appeared in a widely-publicized
and critically-acclaimed Nike television spot
highlighting baseball and football star Bo
Jackson). Nike marketing director David
Kottkamp was clearly happy with his company's association with the hockey star,
which began in 1983.

"Like Michael Jordan and John
McEnroe," raved Kottkamp, "Wayne Gretzky
is bigger than his sport."

8

The Champion

HEADING INTO THE 1982–83 SEASON, Wayne Gretzky had everything a twenty-one-year-old could want—and more. He had fame, fortune, family, the respect and admiration of his peers, and the love of an entire country. The only thing he didn't have was a championship ring.

The Oilers were gearing everything this season toward further solidifying their maturing team and, ultimately, taking the Stanley Cup away from the New York Islanders, who had won three straight championships and were clearly the class of the league. With players like Jari Kurri, Mark Messier, Glenn Anderson, and Paul Coffey developing into stars, Edmonton's brass felt the opposition wouldn't be able to concentrate solely on stopping Gretzky (which they really couldn't do anyway). The Oilers believed their top players could certainly be a match for the Islanders' superstar contingent of Mike Bossy, Bryan Trottier, and Denis Potvin. They also believed that Grant Fuhr was developing into the kind of goalie who could stop pucks with the flair, if not the pugnaciousness, of the Islanders' Billy Smith.

But Edmonton would have to get through an 80-game season and three playoff series before taking on the Islanders. The season proved to be little problem. Now a certified NHL power, the Oilers finished first in the Campbell Conference with a 47–21–12 record, 28 points ahead of second-place Calgary in the Smythe Division. They scored an astounding 424 goals and registered 1129 assists, to set NHL team records in both categories. The Oilers also set a league record for having the most 40-plus goal scorers in one season, with four. Aside from Gretzky, Anderson scored 48 goals and 104 points, Messier scored 48 goals and had 106 points, and Kurri chipped in with 45 goals and 104 points. On defense, Coffey, already one of the league's best backliners, continued to establish himself as an offensive force, notching 29 goals and 67 assists.

As for Gretzky, well, he was Gretzky. He couldn't top his goal-scoring output of the

'81–82 season, netting "only" 71, but he still managed to set another assist record, with 125, for a league-leading 196 points overall and win his third straight Art Ross Trophy. Wayne also was awarded his fourth successive Hart Trophy as Most Valuable Player and was again the Lester B. Pearson award-winner. It was just another typically great year for The Great One.

But it didn't turn out to be another typical playoff year for the Edmonton Oilers. There would be no early-round upset knockouts against them this time, as they dispatched Winnipeg, Calgary, and the Chicago Black Hawks in just 12 games, setting up a final-round confrontation with the Islanders.

While the Oilers were showering the defending champions with the appropriate respect ("Some of our guys haven't even played pro hockey as long as they've been winning Stanley Cups," said Glen Sather), the men from Long Island were expressing their disdain for the flashy scoring machine from Edmonton. "We want to beat them more than anything," said Islander forward Clark Gillies. "You know why? Because they think they're the greatest thing since sliced bread." Teammate Bob Bourne chimed in with: "The Oilers are so damn cocky. The thing that really bugs me is that they don't respect us. All the other good teams respect us, but Edmonton doesn't respect anyone. There isn't any team we want to beat more. If we win, it will be the sweetest victory we've ever had."

The last thing Gretzky wanted to do was add fuel to this particular fire. He didn't want to give the Islanders any more incentive. "We're confident, but we're not cocky," Wayne contended. "That's what got us into trouble against L.A. last year. We think we can win this, but we also know we have to prove it on the ice. We're not going to win this thing by out-talking people. We'll do it by outskating, outhitting, outchecking, and outworking them. And not too many teams have done that to the Islanders."

And the Oilers didn't do that to the Islanders this year, either. Billy Smith's great goaltending made two New York goals stand up in the first game, and the Islanders took the second game in Edmonton easily, 6–3. "We couldn't have made it much harder for ourselves," Gretzky moaned. "You don't come back against great teams when you get too far into a hole."

Again the kid was right. Back at the Nassau Coliseum the teams battled in a 1–1 game before the Islanders blew it open in the third to win 5–1. The chant of "sweep" was echoing through the Coliseum when the fourth game began, and the Islanders didn't waste any time responding to their home fans' desires. They took a 3–0 lead in the first period, gave back two in the second, and took their fourth straight Cup when Ken Morrow scored into an empty net in the third. The Islanders' experience—11 regulars between twenty-eight and thirty-two—triumphed over the Oilers' youth and firepower.

"We didn't lose to a good team, we lost to a great team," said a disheartened Gretzky, who led all Stanley Cup scorers with 26 assists and 38 points, set a record for most short-handed goals in a playoff year with three, but was successfully muzzled by the Islanders. "I envy them and respect the way they do things. When they were celebrating, their guys had ice packs on their shoulders, their jaws, their knees. We can learn a lot from the Islanders about what it takes. Putting your face in front of slapshots, taking a punch in the face, sacrificing—that's what it takes to win."

Though the Oilers had been swept, it was obvious to everyone in the hockey world that this was a team on the verge of greatness. With the experience of playing in a final series, Edmonton was regarded as a serious Cup challenger for the 1983–84 season. In fact, many experts thought this was a team that could not only beat the aging Islanders, but possibly establish a dynasty just as impressive.

Speaking of impressive, what other word could be used to describe the Oilers' regular season performance in 1983–84? Edmonton totally dominated the league with a 57–18–5 mark, setting another team scoring record with 446 goals. Jari Kurri was a 50-goal scorer, Paul Coffey scored 40 goals and added 86 assists (a remarkably high total for a defenseman) to finish second in the scoring race behind—who else?—The Great One. Wayne didn't break any of his previous regular-season scoring records, but might have had he not missed six games with minor injuries. His 87 goals, 118 assists, and 205 points earned him the Art Ross and Lester Pearson trophies again, and he silenced critics of his defensive play by winning the Emory Edge Award for having the league's best plus-minus rating. But Wayne Gretzky wouldn't let a season go by without getting his name into the record books. This year he would set the NHL marks for most shorthanded goals in a season (12), the longest consecutive assist-scoring streak (17), and the longest consecutive point-scoring streak (51), the latter also setting a record for doing it from the start of a season. And, of course, Gretzky won another Hart Trophy as the league's MVP. At this point it would have made sense to engrave his name on the Hart about ten more times and just let it sit in his house, which already contained enough hardware to fill a museum.

But more than anything else in the world, Wayne Gretzky wanted to see his name engraved on a Stanley Cup. If ever the Oilers were primed to strike championship crude, it was now. The bad blood that began boiling in last year's finals carried over into this one, but now it was Edmonton that was raging with dislike for the New Yorkers. The Oilers were tired about hearing how the Islanders couldn't lose, and they wanted to stop New York's "drive for five" right in its tracks.

The finals would also be a personal challenge for Gretzky, who was being maligned in the media for not scoring much in the '83 series. The press, especially the New York press, kept implying that he couldn't hack it under playoff pressure and asked whether Wayne was "really great or not." Wayne worried that if Edmonton lost again and he failed to have a spectacular series, he would be thought of as just a great regular-season player, not a great all-around player. He hoped another seven-game series would prove he could hack it in the big games.

The opener in Nassau Coliseum was practically a must game for the Oilers. Usually, teams want to split the first two games in the other guy's arena, but Edmonton desperately needed a psychological edge after the previous year's four-game blowout. If they could take Game One on the road, momentum would be established and the Islanders' image of invincibility would be a tad tarnished.

Battlin' Billy Smith was very tough in the Islander goal throughout the game, but Grant Fuhr, who had had his best season as the

Oiler goalie, was even better. Fuhr was extremely aggressive, coming far out of his net to cut down the angles. When the Oilers' Kevin McClelland put a quick shot by Smith in the first period, everyone in the Edmonton camp seemed confident Fuhr could make it hold up. The Islanders threw everything they had at the young goalie but couldn't solve him. Game One went to the Oilers, 1-0.

"All we needed was a game like this to prove to ourselves—and to them—that we could win a tight one," said Gretzky after the game. He was ecstatic even though the Islanders had shut him down again. "The Islanders have been the team that wins these games, and we've been the one that makes that one disastrous mistake. But it didn't happen this time because we've got a new attitude. We think we can win any kind of game, and we proved that tonight. But the Islanders are one of the greatest teams ever and they know what it takes to come back."

And come back the Islanders did in Game Two, dominating the Oilers from the opening face-off. After Edmonton lost 6-1, the Canadian media began writing them off, predicting the Oilers would blow another playoff series, as they had in the past. But as Gretzky kept saying, this was a different team, a more mature team, one that wouldn't succumb easily to playoff pressure. And the next three games would be in the friendly surroundings of the Northlands Coliseum.

The Oilers were down 2–1 halfway through Game Three's second period when Mark Messier sent a wrist shot past Smith to tie the game. It turned out to be the goal that changed the direction of the series. Messier, his teammates, and the Oiler fans went wild with jubilation. Edmonton started skating like a team possessed. They scored two goals at the end of the second, so demoralizing the Islanders that New York completely fell apart in the third period. The final was 7–2, Edmonton. Everybody—the players, the fans, the media—realized they had witnessed a turning point in the team's history.

The Oilers had not only won, they won without Gretzky being the dominant player on the ice. Their momentum clearly carried over into the next game, in which the Oilers blew the Islanders out again, 7–2. Gretzky scored on a breakaway and was finally getting into a groove he hoped would lead his team to a Game Five victory. And he desperately wanted to win the Cup in front of the home fans.

"It's been very hard not to get too anxious, not to get so wound up thinking about what one more win means," Gretzky said before Game Five. "But I just keep thinking that if we let up even a little bit, we could be going

back to Long Island. And we just don't want
to give that team that kind of chance."

Wayne personally saw to it that the Cup
would be won in Edmonton. He scored the
first two goals and inspired the Oilers to a
two-period domination of the game. Grant
Fuhr was stopping everything, and when the
teams left the ice after two, it was 4–0 Edmonton, a seemingly insurmountable deficit for
any team, even the Islanders.

But these were the four-time Stanley Cup
champions, and they weren't about to go
down without a fight. No sooner had the puck
been dropped at the start of the third period
than the Islanders scored two goals, both by
Pat LaFontaine, at the 13- and 45-second
marks. Now New York would have more than
enough time to take the game. But Grant
Fuhr never lost his composure, and the Oiler
defense stiffened. They stopped the Islanders
cold for the remaining 19 minutes, 15 seconds, and Edmonton had its first Stanley Cup.

In the joyous locker room Wayne Gretzky
probably had more champagne poured over
his head than he had ever drunk in his whole
life. In 19 playoff games he had scored 13
goals and assisted on 22 others. His season
goal total, including playoffs, was 100, which
set an NHL record. He also set a record for
most shorthanded goals in a playoff year with
three. But on the day people danced through
the streets of Edmonton, Wayne Gretzky

wasn't thinking about personal accomplishments or individual records. He was feeling what it was like to be a Stanley Cup champion.

"This is better than I ever imagined it would feel," The Great One gushed. "You work all year, you work for years, you work all your life, to experience this moment."

It was the first such moment for Wayne Gretzky in his young career, but surely it wouldn't be his last.

9

The Dynasty Builder

LED BY THEIR SUPERSTAR in 1984–85, the Oilers breezed through the regular season and the first three rounds of the playoffs. For the fourth straight season Wayne led the NHL in goals, assists, and points. He scored just 73, but, naturally, set another new assist record with 135. He also led the league again in shorthanded goals with 11 and won his fifth straight MVP award.

But if there was one thing still nagging at Wayne, one thing he hadn't felt he'd yet accomplished, it was being a dominant force in a Stanley Cup final. Oh, sure, he'd led playoff scorers in points two years in a row, but the Islanders had been pretty much able to stifle him in the '83 and '84 finals. So going into the '85 finals against the Philadelphia Flyers, Wayne felt he had something to prove.

As in the two previous years, he got off to a slow playoff start, but so did the entire Oiler team. Though Edmonton was favored to take their second straight Cup, the Flyers didn't seem impressed, and won the first game 4–1. But the Oilers regrouped, and with Fuhr on top of his game, Edmonton took Game Two 2–1. As for Gretzky, he may not have been scoring much, but everyone was noticing a subtle difference in his style of play. He was skating hard on both ends of the ice, playing superb defense, and exuding more leadership than he'd ever shown before. "The way Gretz was playing," observed Kevin Lowe, "it was only a matter of time before he got going offensively."

In Game Three it took Gretzky only about two minutes, to be precise. Invigorated by the Edmonton crowd, he scored two goals 15 seconds apart in the first 100 seconds of the first period, and notched a third goal later in the opening stanza. The Flyers struggled to come back, but the Oiler defense held off the charge for a 4–3 victory. Philadelphia jumped to an early 3–1 lead in Game Four, but the Oilers tied it early in the second period. With a commanding lead in the series in sight, Gretzky took over the game, scoring the next two Oiler goals in a 5–3 triumph that showed Edmonton was not only a team of talent, but of character. The Flyers, now demoralized and burnt out from trying to keep pace with Edmonton's flyers on the ice, went down easily in Game Five, 8–3, and Oiler fans celebrated another Stanley Cup.

"Winning again proves so many things to us and to everyone else," Gretzky said at a New York luncheon at which he accepted the Conn Smythe Trophy as the playoffs' Most Valuable Player. "I think because we are young and balanced and have excellent coaching and management, we can stay on top for a long time. I'm not saying we will do it. I'm saying I think we have the team to do it. We have the experience now, and we know what it takes to win."

The Oilers wanted to create a new hockey dynasty, and Wayne Gretzky wanted to be its master builder. Edmonton wasn't just shooting to be the third straight team to win four Cups in a row (also achieved by the 1976–79 Montreal Canadiens and the 80–83 Islanders), but they wanted to at least match the Canadiens' record of five successive Cups, which Montreal had pulled off between 1956 and 1960.

Once again the Oilers dominated the league. In 1985–86, they produced the NHL's best record with 56 wins and 119 points. Gretzky scored just 52 goals, his lowest total since his second year in the league, but Wayne wouldn't let a "poor" goal-scoring season stand in the way of setting more records. Instead of piling up the goals for himself, he was creating them for his teammates. Of the Oilers' 426 goals, Gretzky assisted on an astounding 163, which not only broke his own assist record by ten, it set a new point-scoring record with 215. And guess which trophies The Great One won? Tough question, isn't it? Wayne took home his two favorites, the Art Ross and the Hart, and prepared to lead the Oilers to their third straight Cup.

After cold-cocking the Vancouver Canucks in the first round, the Oilers went up against the Calgary Flames, their sister city in Alberta, the Smythe Division runner-up and a team Edmonton had beaten six out of seven times with one tie during the regular season. But Calgary had been improving as the season progressed, and the game they beat the Oilers had been the last one between the two teams. Spurred on by the rivalry talk of sportswriters and fans, the Flames were hungry to establish their identity, and they proved it in the first game of the Smythe semifinal, winning 4–1. The Oilers came back in Game Two, and over the next four games the teams traded victories to set up a Game Seven in Edmonton.

Though the series had already gone longer than anyone expected, the Oilers and their fans were confident that the Flames would be doused in the final game and that

Edmonton would continue its date with Stanley Cup destiny. But it wasn't meant to be. Calgary took a 2–0 lead and Edmonton fought back to tie it. But midway through the third period there occurred the kind of fluke incident that can decide championships. Edmonton's young defenseman Steve Smith skated with the puck behind his own goal and prepared to set up the play down ice. But instead of making a crisp pass, the puck trickled off his stick, hit goalie Grant Fuhr on the back of the leg, and went into the net for Calgary's go-ahead goal. Gretzky couldn't perform any miracles this time, and Edmonton went down 3–2 in a stunning upset that ended their Stanley Cup streak.

In the wake of this devastating defeat, Wayne Gretzky revealed more aspects of his development as a person. Not only had he reached a level of maturity beyond his twenty-five years, but he had developed a level of class rarely seen in professional sports. All this was crystallized in the way he helped young Steve Smith deal with a mistake which at first had the kid in tears on the bench and then left him distraught in the locker room. After the game Wayne took Smith aside and talked with him privately for several minutes. He let the kid know that it would be futile and destructive to blame himself for the loss. Then, without revealing details of the conversation, Gretzky spoke to the media:

"One play doesn't decide a series, and Steve played exceptionally well all through this series," Gretzky said in support of his teammate. "The Oilers lost this series to the Flames. Steve Smith is a member of this team and so am I and another twenty guys in here who are responsible. We all lost."

The Oilers didn't let the unexpected Stanley Cup loss of '86 get them down the following season. With the best nucleus of talent in hockey—all the main characters, Messier, Kurri, Coffey, Fuhr, were now as established as superstars as Gretzky—the Oilers again compiled the league's best record in 1986–87, with 106 points, 11 more than the division runner-up, the Calgary Flames.

What made some Oiler observers nervous about the playoffs, however, was the fact that the Flames' victory over the Oilers in the previous year's playoffs seemed to carry over into the new season. With a 6–1–1 record against Edmonton, Calgary had reversed last year's regular-season mark between the teams, and the two clubs were now heated rivals.

As for Gretzky, great seasons were now becoming commonplace. He led the league in goals (62), assists (121), and points (183) for the fifth time in his eight-year NHL career. There were no big regular-season records this year, but he did grab the Art Ross, Hart, and Lester Pearson awards again, and had the best plus-minus ratio for the third time in four years. On November 22 he reached a milestone by scoring his 500th goal, doing it approximately 200 games faster than anyone in NHL history.

When Wayne hit the 500 mark, it generated a whole new wave of verbal tributes about him. Hockey people always seemed to be looking for ways to describe The Great One's amazing ability, as if talking about it could make them understand it. Former Toronto Maple Leaf player and coach Howie Meeker said that "Gretzky is beyond comparison. He's in a class by himself." And when some people began to suggest that Pittsburgh Penguin phenom Mario Lemieux, who had scored over 100 points in his first two seasons, was better than Gretzky, Meeker told the *Edmonton Sun* that "Lemieux can't carry Gretzky's jockstrap."

"I've looked, but I just can't find a weakness in him," admitted the great Bobby Orr, who was credited with revolutionizing hockey years before Gretzky, and retired the year Wayne arrived in the NHL, 1979. "They say he can't play defense, but you don't have to when you have the puck all the time. There are great players in the game, but no one can even compare."

And speaking for all NHL goalies, Hartford's Mike Liut simply said, "Wayne Gretzky doesn't play fair."

After knocking out the Los Angeles Kings

in five games in the opening playoff round, the Oilers prepared for another tough series with the Flames. But the Winnipeg Jets got in the way of another meeting between these intense rivals when they upset Calgary in six games. Though they were pumped up for the Flames ("losing to them has been on our minds all year," said Gretzky), the Oilers didn't let down against the weaker opponent and downed the Jets in four straight. Beating the Detroit Red Wings in five for another Campbell Conference championship meant a rematch of the 1985 finals with the Philadelphia Flyers.

As everyone predicted, the final featured hard-hitting, tight-checking, frantic-skating hockey. In the first game the Oilers led 2–1 before Gretzky put the game out of reach with a magnificent pass to set up a Paul Coffey goal. "We knew we couldn't afford to lose the opener to Philadelphia," Wayne said after the 4–1 win. With the score 0–0 after one period in the second game, Gretzky put the Oilers ahead with a goal after 45 seconds were gone in the third. But Flyers goalie Ron Hextall stopped Edmonton cold for the rest of the period while his team took a 2–1 lead. Hextall held the lead for almost 12 minutes of the third before Glenn Anderson scored to tie it. Then, as Kevin Lowe would remark later, "Gretz demonstrated why he is The Great One." Wayne rushed the puck up ice and into the Flyer zone. Once inside the blue line, he could have shot, but he found Coffey and passed to the defenseman. Coffey then noticed Jari Kurri 15 feet away from Hextall and sent a pass that Kurri put into the open corner of the net, which proved to be the winning goal.

The picture-perfect play appeared to be a momentum builder when the Oilers went ahead 3-0 in Game Three, but the Flyers, always a tough, scrappy bunch, scored five unanswered goals in the last 25 minutes. The Oilers came back to win Game Four 4-1, with the game-winner coming on another great pass from Gretzky to Kevin Lowe. The Oilers now had a chance to win their third Cup on home ice, but as an Edmonton paper proclaimed after Game Five, THE OILERS CHOKED. They had blown a 3-1 lead, which sent the series back to Philadelphia for a Game Six. Gretzky set up Lowe for a 1-0 Oiler lead, but again the Flyers stormed back to take the game, 3-2, and send their fans into a state of ecstasy.

Oiler fans were prepared to erupt when their team took the ice for Game Seven. The pressure was clearly on the home team. If Edmonton didn't win this series, they would go from being labeled a minidynasty to being called major underachievers. Although the Flyers got the game's first goal, the Oilers immediately tied it, then went ahead in the second period when Gretzky set up Jari Kurri for the go-ahead goal. The play invigorated the Oilers. Sensing a victory was in their grasp, they skated the Flyers into the ice and scored a late third-period insurance goal. After the clock read 0:00, Edmonton drank champagne from the Stanley Cup for the third time in four years. As captain of the team, Gretzky had the honor of being the first to skate around the ice with the championship trophy. "I never get tired of carrying this Cup around," he said. "Now we can look for another one."

Winning their fourth Stanley Cup in five years would be made more difficult for the Oilers in 1987–88 because they'd have to do it without All-Star defensemen Paul Coffey. After haggling with Sather and Pocklington over a new contract, Coffey sat out training camp and the beginning of the season rather than sign with Edmonton. Then, in November, the Oilers traded Coffey to the Pittsburgh Penguins (where he would play with another great scorer in Mario Lemieux). The key to the deal for Edmonton was the acquisition of twenty-year-old forward Craig Simpson, who would become a 50-goal scorer for the Oilers.

As for the "franchise," this would be Wayne Gretzky's first NHL season when he wouldn't score at least 50 goals. But it was also the first time he would sustain the kind of injury that would force him to miss a substantial chunk of the season. On December 30 he was hit hard while scoring a goal in a 7–0 victory over the Flyers. The goal was Wayne's 573rd, tying him with Mike Bossy on the all-time list. But the joy over the milestone was tempered when Wayne found he'd suffered a knee sprain that would keep him sidelined until February. The bright side was that he would get a midseason rest for the first time in ten years, enabling him to be fresh when playoff time rolled around.

Once the knee was healthy, it was time for Gretzky to continue his assault at one of the NHL's most revered records: Gordie Howe's lifetime assist mark of 1049. Of course, the fact that Howe was Wayne's childhood idol made the story all the more compelling. Gretzky and Howe were tied when the Oilers played the Penguins in Edmonton on February 19. But a sold-out house was disappointed when, with less than five minutes gone in the first period, Wayne was accidentally hit in the left eye with a Pittsburgh stick and was forced to leave the game. An examination showed Wayne had suffered a corneal abrasion and a bit of hemorrhaging behind the eye which would knock him out of action for a week.

After being shut out by the Flames upon his return, Gretzky scored a goal, his 36th of the year, in the first period of the March 1st game against the Los Angeles Kings. The 16,000 people packing the Northlands Coliseum barely got a chance to stop cheering when, 18 seconds after scoring, Wayne assisted on Jari Kurri's 32nd of the season. Gordie Howe's record was history, so to speak. The game was halted and with the Oiler fans shouting their approval, the NHL presented Gretzky with a Tiffany-crafted mantel clock. The Oiler organization gave him a gold hockey stick and a $50,000 bond payable upon his first child's twenty-first birthday. But the highlight of the moment was the phone message from Howe—who was away doing charity work—which was piped in over the public address system.

"I'm sorry I couldn't be there, but I'm awful happy for you," Howe told Gretzky. "Thank you for allowing me to carry the record for a while. There's no one on earth I'd rather see break it."

What made Gretzky's achievement so awesome was the time in which it took him to do it. Howe compiled 1049 assists over 1767 games. It took Gretzky only 681 games in nine years. After the game, which the Oilers won 5–3, the press asked Gretzky for a comment about breaking such a prestigious record. Wayne used the opportunity to take a jab at the critics who'd knocked him since he joined the NHL.

"When I came into the league, people questioned my consistency," he said calmly. "I think I showed you can be 170 pounds and under six feet and play in this league. Brains are an important part of the game."

Wayne led the league in assists for the ninth straight year, but missing 16 games forced him to turn over the Art Ross and Hart trophies to Mario Lemieux. And for the first time since 1981, the Oilers did not win the division championship, finishing second to the hated Calgary Flames. But, of course, in the wacky world of the NHL, where 16 out of 21 teams make the playoffs, a team could finish third or fourth in a division, play 10 to 20 games under .500, fill a team with minor leaguers, and still win the Stanley Cup. It was a silly system, one which even Gretzky criticized, and when The Great One spoke, people listened, especially the media.

Wayne believed the NHL's playoff format penalized the better teams, since some divisions, like the Smythe, were stronger than others. He wanted to see a conference playoff format, pitting the first-place team against eighth place, two against seven, etc. "We have to do something," he insisted. "Every year Boston has to play Montreal early and we have to play Calgary. That's not right. Good teams like that should be meeting in later rounds. You should reward teams for performance instead of rewarding them for the division they play in.

"It's not fair to the fans or the teams. You get into a series like we had with Calgary two years ago, and it's only seen in Western Canada. That's ridiculous. They don't have to sell hockey in Calgary or Edmonton, but there are other places they have to sell it. The more people watching the better teams, the better it is for the game."

That Gretzky was absolutely right about the NHL playoff system didn't faze the league's greedy, self-centered, small-minded owners. Nothing about the format has been changed and probably won't be until some visionary officials and owners can be recruited to run the league.

The Oilers started off the "second season" well, beating the Winnipeg Jets in five tough games, setting up another hot division final with the Flames. Calgary believed the Oilers were finally beatable, but they put themselves in a hole by losing the first game at home, 3–1. Gretzky had put the game away with a breakaway goal late in the third. In Game Two Calgary blew 3–1 and 4–3 leads and the game went into overtime. For six minutes of the extra session Edmonton's pressure was fierce, until they were called for a two-minute penalty. As part of the penalty-killing unit, Gretzky was on the ice when Kurri sent him a pass along the boards. Wayne streaked down the left side and blasted a shot by Flames' goalie Mike Vernon to win the game. Afterwards, the player who had scored more clutch goals than about half the league, said, "It was the biggest goal I ever scored."

After such a demoralizing loss, and with the series going back to Edmonton, nobody gave Calgary much of a chance. The Oilers, now a mature, experienced, defending Cup champion, weren't about to get caught up in the "sweep" hype. They kept a low profile and focused on the job at hand. It proved to be the right strategy, as the Oilers won Game Three 3–1 and Game Four 6–3. Edmonton had knocked out the number-one team during the regular season, and with 5 goals and 12 assists in his first nine games, Gretzky was having his best playoff year ever.

In the Campbell Conference championship against the Detroit Red Wings, Edmonton won the first two games before losing the third 5–2. Gretzky scored both Oiler goals but was a target of some fierce body-checking throughout the game. This was not something new for him. He knew that when he was playing, there was somebody trying to decapitate him, so he was always aware of his position on the ice. Wayne always tried to stay out of traffic and away from the corners where the hitting was the heaviest. His peripheral vision and double-jointed feet—which allowed him to skate lower and more bent over than the average player—enabled him to evade a lot of body checks meant for his head. And most opposing players felt justified in handling the NHL's meal ticket this way.

"He's not an untouchable," said Red Wings forward Bob Probert. "I'm sure there are a lot of players who treat him that way, but part of my game is bumping and grinding, and in my eyes he's no different than any other player out there." But Probert was singing a different tune about Gretzky and the Oilers after his team lost Game Four in overtime and were demolished in Game Five 8–4.

Trying to stop Edmonton's quest for their fourth Stanley Cup in five years would be the Boston Bruins, who had just won a tough seven-game series against the surprising New Jersey Devils. Gretzky gave the attending scribes something to write about when he showed up for practice one day wearing a short brush-haircut, reminiscent of the ones worn by rock star Billy Idol and pro football's Brian Bosworth. "Hey, it's just a haircut," Gretzky told the media. "I heard it's hot in Boston Garden."

It was the Oiler defense that was hot in a 2–1 opening-game victory. Steve Smith, the "goat" of the '86 playoffs, assisted on both goals. "He had a great series against Calgary, too," reminded Gretzky, who never wasted an opportunity to pump up the young defenseman. The Oiler defense was merely great in winning Game Two 4–2. Gretzky was his usual dominant self in the second contest, saving one score by kicking a Bruin shot out of the goal crease and getting a couple of assists when Boston penalties gave the Oilers two two-man advantages. Boston hung tough for a period and a half of Game Three before the Oilers' explosive offense took over for a 6–3 victory.

Game Four turned out to be one of the weirdest in NHL history. With the score tied 3–3 and about three minutes remaining in the second period, the lights in Boston Garden went out. The delay was so long that the game was cancelled and the rematch played in Edmonton. Boston took an early 2–1 lead, but couldn't hold it. The Oilers tied the game late in the first period, and scored three second period goals, with Gretzky assisting on the last one, which broke the Bruins' backs. Wrote *Sports Illustrated* after the Oiler victory: "It was more coronation than competition."

For the second time in his career the Great One was named the Conn Smythe Trophy winner as the playoff MVP. Overall, he scored 12 goals and compiled 43 points in the '88 playoffs. In the finals Gretzky set playoff records for most assists (10) and points (13). He also set a new mark for most assists in a playoff year (31).

The Edmonton Oilers may not have won four Stanley Cups in a row, like Montreal and the Islanders, but with four in five years they now had to be considered a hockey dynasty. And if anybody doubted that Wayne Gretzky had been the primary architect of that dynasty, all they had to do was ask the Calgary Flames' Paul Reinhart, who suggested after his team was beaten by the Oilers: "We would have won if we'd had Wayne Gretzky."

"A lot of people counted us out because we lost Coffey and some other top players in one year," Wayne said after the series. "But, you know, all we talked about in the dressing room was the young guys coming up; that they didn't know how exciting it was to be on a winner, and what a great experience it was going to be for them.

"Last year's team was the most talented I've ever played on," he continued. "But this team is the best I've ever played on. We're going to be very tough to beat for a number of years to come. I have four years left on my contract (he had signed that five-year contract in '87), and right now I intend to fulfill that. Of course, you never know what's going to happen down the road, but this year was the most fun I've ever had playing hockey."

And who could predict when the Edmonton dynasty would end? After all, they were led by a guy who was only twenty-seven years old and could play with the Oilers until at least 1992. Did anybody say five Cups? Six? Ten? Only time would tell. But with The Great One, anything was possible.

10

The Married Man

ALL THROUGH HIS YOUNG PROFES-
sional career, people wondered if the world's
greatest hockey player and one-man conglomerate ever set aside enough time for a personal
life. Would he ever get married? And if he did
tie the knot, how would it affect his game?
One thing was for sure: As long as Wayne
Gretzky remained single, there would be hope
for thousands of Canadian girls who dreamed
about being Mrs. Great One.

But there had been a special girl in Wayne
Gretzky's life since 1979, his first year in Edmonton. For eight years one couldn't read a
magazine article about Gretzky without seeing a photo of him with Vickie Moss, the
blond, vivacious, Edmonton-born cutie who

wanted to make it as a pop singer. Wayne had met Vickie at an Edmonton club where she was performing. She knew nothing about sports and didn't know Gretzky was a local celebrity. So when Wayne left her tickets to a hockey game, she gave them to two of her nine brothers. Vickie accepted Wayne's second invitation, and shortly thereafter they began living together.

"She takes me completely away from it all," Wayne said. And his friend, Oiler goalie Eddie Mio, observed: "He's gotta be real careful about the hangers-on, and she's given him stability."

But by 1987 the Gretzky-Moss relationship was becoming strained. Wayne's hockey career, travel abroad, constant personal appearances, and her pursuit of a singing career, meant the couple was spending a lot of time apart. Moss moved to Los Angeles seeking her big break as a performer. When Wayne asked her to return to Edmonton in the spring of '87, she told him she wanted to stay in L.A. for at least another year. Wayne had wanted to get married and was upset by Vickie's decision. "Wayne was so bitter with me," Moss told Canada's *Maclean's* magazine in 1988. "It was a shame he could not handle it."

Right around the time of their breakup, Wayne went to Palm Springs, California, to see Vickie perform. Since he was near Los Angeles, he figured he would meet his friend, television actor Alan Thicke, and take in a Lakers–Boston Celtics National Basketball Association championship game. While at the game, Gretzky ran into actress Janet Jones, a beautiful twenty-six-year-old blonde he had first met in 1981 on the set of the TV show *Dance Fever*. He appeared on the show as a judge, she as a dancer. Nothing came of it then because he was involved with Moss and she was dating Nils Van Patten, the son of TV's Dick Van Patten. But seeing Janet again now, Wayne felt another kind of fever, and he wasn't going to let his second chance get away. During the basketball game he asked her out, and Jones—unattached after a two-year engagement to tennis star Vitas Gerulaitis and a brief fling with *Moonlighting* star Bruce Willis—responded quicker than Gretzky gets off a wrist shot.

"From the first day, we hit it off well," remembered Wayne. "It kind of hits you like a ton of bricks. I knew after the second time I saw her I wanted to marry her, because our chemistry was so strong."

Jones was the youngest daughter in a St. Louis family of seven and was a self-described "tomboy" who wanted to play pro softball. But after becoming proficient in ballet and jazz, she moved to New York at eighteen and got a part in the chorus of a Radio City Music Hall show. After moving to L.A., she was hired for *Dance Fever* and also worked as a model, appearing on the cover of *Life* and *Harper's* and in commercials for Wrangler Jeans, Shasta Cola, and Kodak.

In 1984, Jones was discovered on a tennis court by director Garry Marshall, who gave her a part in his movie, *The Flamingo Kid*, which became a minihit. Good notices in *Kid* earned her a part in the movie version of *A Chorus Line*, a lead role in the 1986 bomb, *American Anthem* (she played a gymnast), and a part as a police officer in *Police Academy V.*

But her most controversial career move came in March 1987, when she appeared on the cover of *Playboy* and posed partially nude inside its pages. Though this didn't bother her new boyfriend one iota ("I think that her life is her life, and what she did before she met me is none of my business," Gretzky told the *Edmonton Journal)*, it ruffled the feathers of the conservative burghers of Alberta, already upset that their Wayne wasn't romancing a nice Canadian girl. "What I don't understand," one citizen wrote to the *Edmonton Sun,* "is why he's dating a *Playboy* bunny when he can have the pick of the crop."

Jones couldn't understand what all the fuss was about. After all, *Playboy* is a prestigious publication, the photos were tasteful, and she didn't show, well, everything. "There wasn't anything embarrassing about what I did," she said. "I wasn't ashamed of any of the pictures, but after I started dating Wayne, I was most concerned about him and his family. The press made me out to be some kind of American playmate. I think Canadians are more conservative than Americans. In the States they didn't think I showed enough."

During the 1987–88 season Wayne was not only playing hockey, he was teaching it— to his new girlfriend. Jones was a complete novice when it came to the game. The first matches she ever saw were the ones during the '87 Canada Cup in September, the series in which Gretzky led Team Canada over the Soviet Union two games to one in the finals. It was a series that Wayne had said during the summer he didn't want to attend. But that was when he was depressed about Vickie and all the career pressures. It was a time when he actually flirted with retiring from hockey.

Janet Jones changed all that. Wayne was clearly smitten with his movie star and wasn't shy about letting people know about it. "She's a great lady," he gushed to the *Edmonton Sun* in December. "It's definitely serious, but obviously right now our minds are on our careers. I don't want to do anything to take her away from pursuing her career. Right now marriage isn't feasible." And in the same interview, Janet added, "We are very much in love and very happy, but marriage, you know, that's in the future." The future turned out to be just one month away, in January, when Gretzky and Jones shocked Canada and the hockey world by announcing their engagement to be married in mid-July. "We were meant to spend our lives together," declared Wayne.

As the wedding date neared and the '88 Stanley Cup finals approached, the Canadian media began to engage in some wacky speculation. Spurred on by Oiler owner Peter Pocklington's comments that Gretzky's play would be adversely affected by his upcoming marriage, the press began predicting that Wayne's performance would deteriorate. They even suggested that his infatuation with Janet had cost him the scoring championship, conveniently forgetting that he missed 16 games because of injury. Wayne was clearly unnerved by the comments. "I didn't need the owner quoted as saying the same things I knew a lot of fans had been thinking," The Great One said bitterly. In his 1988 book *Champions,* written after the '87–88 season, teammate Kevin Lowe said that Jones had "a positive impact on Wayne's life—the impending marriage had given him another reason to want to play well and had enhanced his feelings of security and stability."

By June, Wayne had led the Oilers to their fourth Stanley Cup, and all his attention, and that of Canada, focused on the upcoming wedding. The six-month wait after the engagement announcement and the news that Jones was pregnant—due by year's end—only served to heighten the interest in Edmonton's first couple. With the media coverage of their life becoming more intense, Gretzky and his bride-to-be retreated to Paul Coffey's cottage in Ontario. Then they spent two weeks in Hawaii, just to stay away from the media onslaught as long as possible. "If we had realized the attention it was going to get," quipped Gretzky, "I think we would have eloped."

When July 16, 1988, finally arrived, the consensus in Canada was that the Gretzky-Jones marriage was the most publicized wedding performed in the country since Prime Minister Pierre Trudeau married the mischievous Margaret Sinclair in 1971. "In England they have the royal family," said an Edmonton woman who attended the wedding. "In the United States, it's Hollywood. But we have to make our own heroes in Canada."

The country's national newsweekly, *Maclean's,* covered the affair and featured it on its cover under the title, THE "ROYAL" WEDDING. In its six-page story, *Maclean's* called the wedding "the union of a talented and gentlemanly sports hero who, for many Canadians, embodies some of the nation's most cherished values, and his glamorous American princess." But still, some of Gretzky's countrymen were disturbed by his choice. "Because Wayne

Gretzky is marrying an American girl," said a book editor from Toronto, "there is perhaps a sense that The Great One has not been true to his roots."

Canada's new "royalty" (a description Gretzky reportedly deplored) were married in the late afternoon at St. Joseph's Basilica in Edmonton. About ten thousand people jammed the streets near the Roman Catholic cathedral (which caused a minor controversy, since Gretzky and Jones were both Protestants), many of whom were hoping to see Jones's $40,000 wedding gown, her three-carat, $125,000 diamond engagement ring, or the celebrities among the 600 invited guests and 22-member wedding party. The best man was former Oiler goalie Eddie Mio. Among the guests were Wayne's Edmonton teammates, NHL officials, Alan Thicke, Soviet goalie Vladislav Tretiak ("Wayne's wedding is big news for Russian hockey fans. People are always interested in the lives of stars," he said), and Gordie Howe. "It's a grand day," said Gretzky's idol. "It will be a happy marriage if only he can learn to play hockey."

During the ceremony Wayne seemed a bit nervous and Janet frequently reached for his hand and smiled to reassure him. At the end of their vows, Wayne placed a diamond-studded double band of gold on her finger. For a wedding present The Extravagant One would give his new bride a $250,000 tan-and-cream-colored Rolls-Royce Corniche. Not bad for a twenty-seven-year-old rink rat from Brantford. When the newlyweds emerged from the cathedral, the crowd cheered, silencing the resentment some Canadians felt toward Gretzky over his marrying an American. "We love you, Wayne," they shrieked, as the couple kissed for photographers. Then they were off, headed for Janet's Los Angeles apartment, where Wayne Gretzky's new life as a married man would begin.

11

The Traded One

JUST THREE WEEKS after Wayne and Janet Gretzky were anointed the King and Queen of Canada, they were abruptly deposed. Oh, Gretzky was still a king, all right. But he was now a Los Angeles King. On August 9 the Oilers made one of the biggest, most controversial trades in sports history when they dealt The Great One to Los Angeles. It was a decision that sent all of Canada into complete shock. One minute Gretzky was the idol of millions, the next minute he was gone.

Not since 1977, when the New York Mets baseball team traded beloved pitcher Tom Seaver (who, like Gretzky, was often called The Franchise) had a sports trade so saddened and angered a city or country. And like the Seaver trade, which was sparked by greed, ego, and player-management battles, the Gretzky deal was steeped in controversy. How could it have happened? How could Oiler owner Peter Pocklington trade the player he said in 1987 that he would "adopt in a minute. I'd love to have him as my own son"?

The roots of the trade went back to March, after Gretzky had broken Gordie Howe's assist record and announced his engagement to Janet Jones. Pocklington, who had signed Gretzky to a new five-year contract the previous season, wanted Wayne to renegotiate the deal so it could run two more years. When Wayne declined, the battle, at least in Pocklington's mind, was on. Wayne could sense this immediately. He told linemate Jari Kurri he believed Pocklington would trade him unless he signed a new deal, because he could be a free agent without any compensation going to Edmonton. Rumors began swirling that the owner was listening to offers and shopping Gretzky around.

"Every other contract he [Pocklington] ever had with a player was to his advantage," Gretzky told *Esquire* after he'd left Edmonton. "Until mine. And even though we were a close-knit team, the last two captains before me had been traded. When I was named captain, one of my friends said, 'Well, that ends the streak.' And I said, 'Don't be so sure.'

"It's funny isn't it?" Gretzky continued.

"When an owner makes a business decision, it's just that, a business decision. When a player does the same thing, it's greed."

There was speculation at the time that Pocklington's other businesses were taking a financial beating due to the collapse of the oil and real estate markets. And he still owed the Alberta government $67 million in loans, part of which he secured using Gretzky's contract as collateral. If Pocklington wanted to get back on his financial feet, what better asset did he have than Wayne Gretzky? With a minimum $15 million price tag on Gretzky, coupled with the savings on Wayne's $1.5 million salary, Pocklington could make a cool $22 million by trading his superstar. That's a little less than Vancouver had offered for Gretzky—at least, that's what Wayne's father had found out during the '88 playoffs, but wouldn't tell his son.

A few days after the Gretzky-Jones wedding, Pocklington called the Kings' energetic new owner, Bruce McNall (he had purchased the team after the '88 season from Jerry Buss, who also owns the Los Angeles Lakers of the NBA), and asked if McNall were interested in acquiring Gretzky. That was like asking McNall if he wanted to add the world's best thoroughbred to his stable of horses. Pocklington's $15 million price tag on Gretzky didn't faze McNall a bit. When the Kings' owner called Gretzky on his honeymoon to tell him about the trade talks, Wayne was hurt that Pocklington wouldn't tell him to his face that he was on the market. Wayne now knew his days in Edmonton were numbered. Why would he want to work for a man who wanted to get rid of him? He called his father and told him he would never wear an Oiler uniform again.

The trade negotiations began to pick up more speed than a Gretzky acceleration up ice. Of course, the machinations were kept completely secret from the hockey fans of Canada. On Glen Sather's urging, Pocklington brought the Kings' promising twenty-year-old center Jimmy Carson into the discussions. This was an indication that Sather wasn't completely against the deal, even though he would later tell Gretzky he didn't want the trade made. It wouldn't have surprised Wayne to find out Sather was playing both sides of the fence. After the deal was made, the New York *Daily News* quoted a source as saying that Gretzky viewed Sather, who was also the Oiler general manager, "as a cheapskate who screwed players when it came time to negotiate. Wayne came to despise Sather and Pocklington for the way they treated players."

The hockey trade of the century was consummated early Tuesday morning on August 9. Edmonton sent Gretzky, forward Mike Krushelnyski, and forward Marty McSorley to

Los Angeles for $15 million in cash (part of which, it was later reported, was kicked in by Prime Ticket, the cable TV network that would increase its coverage of Kings games from 37 to 60 with Gretzky as a drawing card), twenty-year-old Jimmy Carson, eighteen-year-old Martin Gelinas—who had been the seventh player taken in the June draft—and the Kings' first-round picks in 1989, '91, and '93. Simply put, Los Angeles traded much of their future for a chance to have The Great One add a Stanley Cup to their present.

Before the hastily called press conference scheduled in Edmonton for that Tuesday morning, Pocklington reportedly gave Wayne a chance to call off the trade. After declining the offer, Wayne also refused to read a prepared statement. Instead, he tearfully told the approximately two hundred reporters that after spending time with McNall, he decided to let the deal go through.

"For the benefit of myself, my new wife, and our expected child [Janet was due in early '89], I decided it would be beneficial for everyone involved to let me play for the Los Angeles Kings. I feel I'm still young enough and capable enough to help a new franchise win the Stanley Cup." After struggling to choke back more tears, he continued, "It's disappointing having to leave Edmonton. I really admire all the fans and respect everyone, but there comes a time when—" Then he stopped, completely overcome with emotion.

Canadian hockey fans, especially those in Edmonton, reacted with a mixture of shock, grief, and anger after the deal was announced. The media, naturally, ate the story up. 99 TEARS, screamed the front page of the *Edmonton Sun*. GRETZKY JUST A PIECE OF MEAT, another paper quoted ex-Oiler Paul Coffey in big headlines. And all the papers and radio talk shows were trashing Janet Jones, claiming she was responsible for turning Wayne against Canada. Jones was called a "witch," a "dragon lady," "Jezebel Janet," and the hockey wife equivalent of Yoko Ono, who had always been blamed for breaking up the Beatles because she was married to John Lennon.

"I expected the other stuff," admitted Jones in *People* magazine. "But when I read that they called me Yoko Ono, I started crying."

Friends immediately jumped to Wayne and Janet's defense. "I'm surprised at all the crap that's coming out," said Paul Coffey. "There's no bloody way Wayne wanted to go to L.A. I don't think the people in Edmonton who know Wayne should believe that. I kind of wished he hadn't broken up at the press conference, and maybe he would have told us what really happened. But he doesn't want to do anything to rock the boat. All he was to the Oilers was a piece of meat." And Gretzky's best man, Eddie Mio, went on Canadian network radio and television and said he couldn't stand to see Janet Jones vilified without cause.

The reactions of Edmonton hockey fans were more heartfelt and echoed the comment of Gretzky's former Oiler teammate Dave Lumley: "Edmonton with Wayne was a glittering city. Edmonton without Wayne is just another city with a hockey team." *Edmonton Sun* columnist Graham Hicks wrote: "He was our best reason for living here." A Canadian politician opined: "Wayne Gretzky is a national symbol, like the beaver. How can we allow the sale of our national symbol? The Oilers without Gretzky is like . . . *Wheel of Fortune* without Vanna White." And an Oiler fan told the *Edmonton Sun:* "I feel like I did when Elvis Presley died."

One of the most poignant reactions came from a Vancouver sports columnist named Jim Taylor, who wrote in *Sports Illustrated,* under the title "A Nation In Mourning": "Forget the controversy over whether No. 99 jumped or was pushed; the best hockey player in the world was ours, and the Americans flew up from Hollywood in their private jet and bought him. It wasn't the Canadian heart that was torn, it was the Canadian psyche that was ripped by an uppercut to the paranoia . . .

" . . . In the minds of Edmontonians and

Canadian hockey fans everywhere, Gretzky had been theirs to keep."

Now Wayne Gretzky belonged to the City of Angels, where reaction to the trade was extremely positive, if not as emotional. The Kings reported receiving 2500 season-ticket requests in the twenty-four hours after the trade was announced, and one of those potential purchasers was Los Angeles Laker basketball star Magic Johnson, who posed for a *Sports Illustrated* cover with Gretzky a few days after the trade was made. "Hey, Wayne belongs in L.A.," Magic insisted. "He's the greatest. Even if the Kings never win a game, it will still be exciting to go see them now."

"I think this is a great day for hockey in L.A.," said Kings' right wing Dave Taylor. "Wayne Gretzky's going to put some people in the seats. We just got the best player in the world."

Two *Los Angeles Times* columnists differed on which team got the better of the deal. In his column, "Deal Is Great One," Scott Ostler wrote: "For about a dozen very solid reasons, the deal might be the Kings' all-time bonehead trade, a sellout of the franchise's future. However, if this is the same Wayne Gretzky I'm thinking of, you can take those dozen reasons, wrap 'em up in a bundle shaped like a large hockey puck, slapshoot the bundle into the L.A. River and watch it drift to sea with the other debris. We got Gretzky. Eat your hearts out, world."

In his column, "Kings Slickered Again by Oilers," Mike Downey wrote: "Hockey is a game of checkers, not chess pieces, but here is one way to look at Tuesday's trade: The Kings got rooked. To get the Franchise, they gave up the franchise. Edmonton saw the Kings coming—as usual. Stripped them clean. Took everything but their jocks and their pucks. Leave it to L.A.'s hopeless hockey team to make a trade for the greatest player who ever lived and still get taken."

Hockey's preeminent writer, Stan Fischler, probably put the deal in the best perspective when he wrote: "If Gretzky brings even one Stanley Cup to California, it will be the best deal the Kings ever made."

On the evening of the historic trade, McNall and the man who would be king of Los Angeles flew back to la-la land for a more upbeat press conference. Before introducing his famous acquisition, McNall said: "Obviously, I'm not doing this to make money. I'm a fan. I want to see hockey become a major league sport in L.A., and this is the way to do it. Ask fifty people in L.A. who Jimmy Carson is, and two or three will know. Ask fifty people who Wayne Gretzky is, and all of them know."

Gretzky smiled as he modeled his new silver and black Kings uniform (they'd switched from purple and gold so they could look less summery and appear as mean as the Los Angeles Raiders football team, who wore the same intimidating colors), and told the assembled media that "it was difficult to leave a city and the people who have become my friends. I hated to leave, and sometimes in life you do things that you don't want to do."

Back in Edmonton, Peter Pocklington was livid. Oiler fans were beginning to let Janet Jones off the hook and were blaming the owner for the departure of their hero. He was hung in effigy in front of the Northlands Coliseum, and fans were threatening to boycott his meat and dairy products in Edmonton. When he saw Gretzky's press conference in Los Angeles, Pocklington freaked.

"Wayne has an ego the size of Manhattan," he told the *Edmonton Journal.* "I understand that, though. If people had told me how great I was every day for ten years, I'm sure my ego would be a pretty generous size, too.

"He's a great actor, too," the owner continued. "I thought he pulled it off beautifully [the Edmonton press conference] when he showed how upset he was. He wants the big dream. I call L.A. the Land of the Big Trip, and he wants to go where the trips are the biggest. If Edmonton fans think their King walked the streets here without ever having a thought of moving, they are under a great delusion.

". . . If Wayne has the integrity I think he has, he'll back up what I said. He could have backed out of the deal just before the press conference started."

"I'm not going to get into a war of words with anybody from Edmonton," Gretzky responded calmly. "But if that's what he thinks, then I'm very disappointed. People who know me and are friends of mine know his statements aren't true."

A few months later, Gretzky told *Esquire*: "When I heard that he said I faked the tears, I was the most pissed off I've ever been at a person in my whole life. Over the past ten years, I had done everything he asked me to do and we'd won four Stanley Cups. For him to throw all that away with one silly remark didn't make any sense."

Janet Gretzky chose not to stay as composed as her husband. "Peter Pocklington is the reason Wayne Gretzky is no longer an Edmonton Oiler," she said. "I know the real story, the whole story, and the story of the trade as presented by Peter Pocklington is false."

One newspaper story seemed to support Janet's contention. On August 12 the New York *Post* reported that the Oiler front office contacted New York Ranger general manager Phil Esposito about a trade for Gretzky in June, long before Pocklington claimed that Gretzky asked out of Edmonton. Esposito said Glen Sather approached him at the NHL

Board of Governors meeting and told him the Oilers "were ready to move Wayne."

The true story of who forced the Gretzky trade probably falls somewhere between Pocklington's version and the Gretzkys' interpretation. Both sides had a vested interest in saving face in front of millions of Canadian hockey fans. Pocklington didn't want the fans to think he cold-heartedly banished "the franchise" for business considerations. Gretzky didn't want his fans to think he wanted to leave them for greener pastures in the U.S. But the Oilers' owner clearly saw the financial benefits in trading his most valuable commodity, especially if he could do it without significantly hurting the team. Wayne was no doubt influenced, if not persuaded, by his bride, to at least consider a trade to the place where she was pursuing her career. And Gretzky and his agents had to realize that the commercial and marketing opportunities for Wayne in Los Angeles would be unlimited. In fact, there were immediate financial benefits, as Gretzky signed a four-year contract extension with the Kings that would take him through the 1995–96 season (as part of the deal, he had the option to retire at least two years before the contract ran out). His money would also be worth more now that he would be getting paid in lesser-taxed U.S. dollars.

But would the deal pay off for the Kings on the ice during the 1988–89 season? Sure,

Gretzky would put more fannies in the seats, but would he put more games in the win column for a team that had never advanced past the second round of the playoffs?

"The trade," said Boston Bruin general manager Harry Sinden, "will bring everyone in the league closer to Edmonton and will bring Los Angeles closer to everyone."

"All of a sudden the Kings have the potential to beat anybody in a short series," observed Calgary Flames' GM Cliff Fletcher. "Anybody that has the greatest player in the world is going to break .500, and Gretzky won't tolerate anything less than winning."

Said Wayne Gretzky, The Great One who was now a King: "Miracles are not going to happen overnight."

12

The King of Kings

NOBODY DOUBTED THAT WAYNE Gretzky was the NHL's best player. Yeah, Mario Lemieux may have won the scoring championship and the MVP award in '88, but he hadn't even come close to leading his team to a Stanley Cup, let alone four. Wayne Gretzky could dominate games. He could bring fans out of their seats with spectacular plays. He could raise the level of his teammates' play. But the question everyone was asking as the 1988–89 season began was: Could he single-handedly turn the Los Angeles Kings into a genuine Stanley Cup threat?

Wayne certainly wouldn't have the kind of supporting cast he had in Edmonton. With Jimmy Carson sent away in the trade, the

Kings' only big scorer was third-year left wing Luc Robitaille, who the previous season scored 53 goals and notched 111 points for fifth place in the NHL scoring race. Eight-year veteran center Bernie Nicholls could be counted on for at least 30 goals. Veteran forward John Tonelli, late of the Flames and Islanders, was signed as a free agent to add more defense up front. Coaching this revised crew of Kings would be 36-year-old Robbie Ftorek, who had taken over midway through the '87–88 season and couldn't get Los Angeles past the division semifinals.

In training camp Gretzky was placed on a line with veteran Dave Taylor and Bobby Carpenter, a former phenom who was trying to reestablish his scoring touch. Everyone knew the Kings would score goals, but their goaltending—Rolland Melanson and Glenn Healy—was considered shaky, their penalty-killing had been weak, and their team defense was erratic. But once he got a look at his new teammates, The Great One was confident the Kings could contend immediately. "I think the team here has the toughness," he said. "It has the talent and the speed. I think we have a better team than people think. This team has more experience than the first few Oiler teams I played on. From what I could see from the outside, no pressure was put on the team from within in the past. This year it's been put on by the owner and the coaches. And there's an extra little bit of pressure because of all the media attention."

But everyone knew the pressure was on Gretzky most of all. If the Kings didn't get off to a good start, the fans would stay home and McNall would take a lot of heat for making a deal that mortgaged the future. "We've got to help Wayne out because he's kind of on the spot," Bernie Nicholls said. "If we don't win here, that's going to make things tough for him. Wayne is the greatest player I've ever seen. If he doesn't bring out the best in us, no one will."

Gretzky didn't wait long to show Nicholls, the Kings, and their fans what he could do for a team. The opening-night crowd at the L.A. Forum for the game against the Detroit Red Wings was a sellout of 16,005, the first sellout for a home opener in the Kings' 22-year history. Before the game the crowd sent a chill through the arena with their thunderous ovation for The Great One. Kings' owner Bruce McNall led the league in goose bumps that night. "Now I know how the guy who was directing *Gone With the Wind* must have felt when he signed Clark Gable to a contract," he said.

As for the state of Wayne's pregame nerves, he would relate later: "I was so excited, so pumped up. The only time I was this nervous before a game was my first All-Star game."

After the Kings fell behind with five minutes gone in the first period, Gretzky took over. He dominated the ice during a Kings' two-man advantage and converted a Dave Taylor pass for his first goal in L.A. and the team's first of the season. His goal ignited the entire Kings' team. Robitaille knocked in a rebound off a Gretzky shot later in the period, scored another goal in the second and nailed a hat trick in the third, scoring on a nifty pass from The Great One, who had three assists. Final score: Kings 8, Red Wings 2.

"It was a lot of fun," Robitaille gushed after the game. "The spirit on this team is unbelievable. You know Wayne is going to work hard on every shift. It was fun to bounce off him. You always get chances when you play with him, so you just go and get those rebounds."

When Detroit goalie Greg Stefan, who could stop only 32 of 40 shots, was asked if any team had ever come at him so relentlessly, he said, "Yes, Edmonton with Wayne Gretzky." And Red Wing coach Jacques Demers was equally impressed with the new-look Kings. "There's a lot of talent on that team, but Gretzky is going to make every player on that team better. When was the last time you saw Carpenter play with that enthusiasm? Nicholls had what, ten hits? They embarrassed us."

Gretzky dealt with the jitters again two

weeks later, when he faced his former team-mates for the first time—in Edmonton. The game at the Coliseum was sold out for months, and 17,503 people went through the turnstiles, making it the Oilers' largest crowd ever. Scalpers were getting forty dollars for a $6.50 ticket. Over 250 media people felt it historic enough to be there, and *Hockey Night in Canada* was televising it as a midweek special. And all anyone wondered about was the kind of reception The Great One would receive from his former fans and how Wayne would react.

"I'd really rather not have to play this game," Gretzky admitted. "We were the closest team, I think, that's ever been assembled in pro sports. It's going to be extremely tough."

"The national anthem will be difficult for him," Walter Gretzky said.

As the crowd waited for the pregame skate, some held up banners that read: BACK IN BLACK, and DOWN THE DRAIN WITHOUT WAYNE. When Gretzky finally stepped out on the Coliseum ice for the first time in an enemy uniform, the fans gave him an ovation lasting nearly four minutes. The crowd cheered when he took his first shift, when he touched the puck for the first time, and when he assisted on two goals. But the Oiler fans could afford to be gracious to The Great One on this night, because their team won the game 8–6.

"Everybody's talked about it for so long now, that I'm happy it's over," Gretzky said after the game. "It was tough for me, and it was just as tough for those guys [his teammates]. It was a hard night for everyone."

There would be much better nights ahead for the Kings and the entire National Hockey League thanks to Mr. Gretzky, resident savior. By mid-November, the Kings were 12–7 (their best start in years), in second place in the Smythe Division behind the Calgary Flames and ahead of, that's right, the Edmonton Oilers. And when the Kings played away games, Gretzky was proving to be the king of the road, fattening the coffers of opposing teams with his ability to bring out the fans. The Kings, who had been one of the NHL's worst draws, saw their road attendance jump 11 percent over their first eight away games. Half the road games were sellouts, and the additional revenue for teams hosting the Kings totalled over $325,000 in tickets and concessions. When two games in Winnipeg against the Kings drew 7000 more fans than the team's games had the previous season, Jets' public relations director Murray Harding observed, "There's no question that Gretzky helped."

The Great One was still the best promoter and marketing man the NHL ever had. "You couldn't clone or develop a better ambassador for your sport," said Capitals' general manager David Poile. "From what I've been told, he's the number-one guy of all the number-one guys in professional sports. That's in terms of presence, how he deals with the public, how he deals with the media."

But Wayne resisted the temptations of Hollywood that would interfere with his concentration on hockey. After arriving in L.A., he was invited to make a guest appearance on the NBC-TV show *Alf,* which was his favorite show, but Wayne turned the producers down. "After I was traded here, I made a decision not to do anything like that off the ice, at least for a while. It's not why I came here."

On the ice Gretzky was a greater influence on his teammates than he'd ever been in the Edmonton years. After their first 37 games the Kings were 24–12–1 and were third in the league in points, behind only Calgary and Montreal. At least half a dozen players were having their best seasons, especially Bernie Nicholls, who had five more goals in his first 37 games than he had all of the '87–88 season. Gretzky's former Oiler teammate, Marty McSorley, noticed that Wayne had become more assertive in the locker room, that he was willing to take the responsibility of leadership.

"He says things now that he didn't say in Edmonton," McSorley said. "Those guys came of age together, they knew what to expect from each player. Here, we don't know what to expect from everybody. With the Oilers, you knew when he was disappointed in the guys. He would just look at you—he'd let you know, but he wouldn't point fingers. He's talking more here. He's stressing the team, the commitment—factors that will be important down the road in the 2–1 and 3–2 games."

But while the Kings were winning games and converts throughout the league, there was talk of controversy in the Los Angeles locker room. In November reports began circulating in the press that the relationship between Gretzky and Robbie Ftorek was becoming strained and that many of the Kings' players disliked their young coach. Jay Wells, who was traded by the Kings to the Philadelphia Flyers early in the season, told *The Hockey News* that Ftorek didn't want Gretzky because Ftorek "can't take a back seat. He's got to be in the limelight. He wants guys who don't say anything . . . because he thinks he's God."

There were rumors of a heated argument between Gretzky and Ftorek after a game in Detroit in which Gretzky notched his 600th career goal and had five assists. But he'd committed a defensive error which led to a late second-period Red Wing goal, and Ftorek benched his superstar for almost eight minutes of the third period.

Publicly, Gretzky and Ftorek denied there was a problem. "I miss a shift and everyone panics," Gretzky said. "Big, small, or indifferent, whatever happened or didn't happen, we'd like to keep it within the team," Ftorek said. But sources later told the press that after the game an angry Ftorek justified the Gretzky benching by saying, "It's my job to teach people things. I'm here to teach." To which Wayne reportedly replied, "If you want to be a teacher, go to New Haven [a minor league team]. I'm here to win a Stanley Cup."

It had become obvious to people around the Kings that Wayne was unhappy with his ice time. Ftorek's coaching philosophy was to treat everybody on the team equally, a silly approach with a player of Gretzky's stature and ability. "To me, to us, Wayne's another hockey player," Ftorek told New York *Newsday* in mid-November. "He happens to be the best there is, but Wayne comes to practice and works like everybody else. When Wayne's up, he plays, same as everybody else. When we say that, everybody thinks we're crazy, but that's the way we see it."

During the second week of December, *Newsday* reported that Gretzky talked owner Bruce McNall out of firing Ftorek at the time of the benching incident. Wayne thought that making a coaching change in midseason would disrupt the team, and if Ftorek was canned, Gretzky would probably be painted as the villain. So Ftorek's job was safe, as long as the Kings kept winning. (Ftorek would be dismissed at the end of the season and replaced by Tom Webster.)

The Kings felt confident about making the playoffs, but the front office knew that for the team to advance past clubs like Edmonton and Calgary, they would need a top-notch goaltender. So on February 22, Los Angeles made a deal second only to the Gretzky trade in its impact. They picked up the young but experienced Kelly Hrudey from the New York Islanders for two prospects, one being goalie Mark Fitzpatrick. Hrudey paid immediate dividends, losing only four of 16 games after the trade and leading the Kings to a second-place Smythe Division finish behind the Flames.

As for The Great One, well, he had another awesome season. He scored 54 goals and had a league-tying 114 assists for 168 points, but finished second to Mario Lemieux in the scoring race for the second straight season. Wayne also tied another impressive record by having a 50-goal season for the ninth year (held also by Mike Bossy). And despite not winning the Art Ross, he was acknowledged for his leadership of the Kings by being voted the Hart Trophy as MVP for a record ninth time in ten seasons. He was also named MVP of the All-Star Game.

But personal achievements had to be the furthest thing from The Great One's mind once the regular season ended. He knew he had to get mentally prepared for one of the greatest challenges of his career, because he would be leading the Kings into the divisional semifinals against his old teammates—the Edmonton Oilers. Wayne knew that, in many ways, this would be the most intense playoff series he'd ever been in.

"The cheering is over," Gretzky said, when asked his feelings about playing for a Stanley Cup with Edmonton as an opponent. "The formalities and the friendships are over. They're the enemy now, and they expect to be the enemy. The guys over there feel the same way."

The Kings suffered a bad break right off the bat when Kelly Hrudey came down with a flu that kept him out of the first game in Los Angeles. Oiler goalie Grant Fuhr was sensational, the defense shut Gretzky down, and Edmonton won 4–3. With a win in Game Two a must, Hrudey was back in goal and Gretzky was back on his game. The Great One assisted on the first goal of the game, then scored in the second period to give L.A. a commanding 4–1 lead. The Kings' fans went wild when it was announced Gretzky had tied Maurice Richard for second place in playoff goals with 82. The Kings' 5–2 win sent the series back to Edmonton tied at 1–1.

When Gretzky took the ice for Game Three in Edmonton, he was greeted by a standing ovation. The crowd was sprinkled with fans wearing black and silver King jerseys with Gretzky's number 99 on the back. But the cheers were just as loud when only ten seconds into the game Wayne missed a scoring chance on a breakaway. Then a happy roar swept through the crowd when Glenn Anderson bodied Edmonton's former hero. There were derisive chants every time Mark Messier, who checked his friend relentlessly, rode Gretzky into the boards. And the fans booed Gretzky the three times Grant Fuhr robbed him in the second period with sensational saves. To put it simply, for Wayne the game was an out and out bummer, and the Kings lost 4–0. His frustration intensified even more when the Kings dropped Game Four, 4–3. "It hasn't been much fun," Gretzky said after the team returned to Los Angeles for Game Five. "The Oilers deserve to be up 3–1, but they haven't dominated us."

It was obvious Gretzky wasn't having a good series, and people wondered why. It turned out it wasn't only Mark Messier's checking and Grant Fuhr's goaltending, but the same flu bug that had bitten Hrudey and John Tonelli. "Nobody knows about it, but Gretz has had the flu," revealed Marty McSorley before Game Five. "He's been feeling pretty crummy. But there's no way Gretz is going to take himself out of the lineup; he cares too much about the team to do that."

Hrudey was back to full strength now and showed it, making unbelievable saves in the third period, when Edmonton tried to tie the game after falling behind 3–2. Then Gretzky, like all great champions who have the killer instinct, put the game away by sending a blistering slapshot past Fuhr. "I'm never comfortable in a game Wayne Gretzky is in," said Oiler coach Glen Sather afterwards, suddenly worried about an L.A. comeback in the series. "Look at the goal Wayne scored to finish us off. He'd been out there on the ice for over four minutes and was dog tired, but he shot off a rocket for that fourth goal."

The momentum of the series had swung to the Kings, but Edmonton was still up by a game and would be at home for Game Six. But that didn't seem to faze the upstart Angelenos. Great goaltending is the great equalizer in the NHL playoffs. Hrudey allowed an Edmonton goal after only 33 seconds had elapsed, but didn't lose his composure. In fact, the goal seemed to make him tougher, and the Oilers couldn't solve him the rest of the night. Meanwhile, Hrudey's teammates were playing what Edmonton's Jimmy Carson would call "an almost perfect game." Mike Allison tied the score late in the second period, and the Kings put three more behind the suddenly beatable Grant Fuhr in the third. With the 4–1 victory, the Kings had broken Edmonton's streak of 14 straight home playoff wins and stood a chance of being only the sixth team in playoff history to overcome an 0-3 or 1-3 deficit and win a series.

"The Forum's going to be rocking," Gretzky said after the game. "Now we can go back home and win it all down there."

Los Angeles was suddenly Hockeywood for Game Seven. With a miracle in the air, the stars came out. Magic Johnson sent balloons to the Kings' locker room, and among those seen yelling support from the stands were actress Kathleen Turner and actors Jack Nicholson and Sly Stallone. But the biggest star in the building on this night would be—who else?—The Great One.

Except, of course, for those Stanley Cup finals games in Edmonton, there were few contests in Wayne's career he wanted to win more than this one. Beat Peter Pocklington? The idea had to give him pleasure, especially after the Oilers' owner said after Game Three that people in Edmonton told him they liked the Gretzky trade.

When the Kings stepped out on the ice, the sellout crowd of 16,005 went berserk. They were still cheering when, about 45 seconds into the first period, Gretzky and Marty McSorley broke in two-on-one against Fuhr. Gretzky faked a cross-ice pass, skated toward the net and shot a change-up that fooled Fuhr, bounced off his pads and rolled into the net. Jari Kurri tied the game four minutes later, but the Kings' Chris Kontos scored his eighth goal in seven playoff games to make it 2–1.

The game was tied 3–3 late in the second period when John Tonelli sent a slapper past Fuhr for a power-play goal. Or so everyone thought. The referees said they did not see the puck go in and disallowed it. Television replays showed that the shot hit the pipe that runs down the back of the goal and bounced out. But just seconds later the Oilers were called for another penalty, giving the Kings a five-on-three advantage. Everybody in the arena could sense what was coming. You just can't give Wayne Gretzky that much open ice. He'll either score himself, or skate around and through the defense until he finds somebody. And he found Bernie Nicholls at 16:23 to give the Kings a 4–3 lead after two periods.

The Oilers skated frantically in the third period, but nothing could get by Hrudey. Late in the period Kevin Lowe knocked his own net off its moorings in an attempt to get his team a breather. All he got was a delay-of-game penalty, and the Kings had their chance for an insurance goal. With the clock ticking their fifth Stanley Cup hopes away, Edmonton pulled Fuhr from the net with two minutes left. It was time for some poetic justice. The clock read 1:40 when Wayne Gretzky grabbed the puck at center ice. Five seconds later he scored into an open net.

"Right now I feel a lot of mixed emotions," Gretzky said after the comeback was completed. "I didn't enjoy playing this series. I saw those guys every day, and yet we didn't speak. That's not what life is supposed to be about. You're supposed to be able to talk to your best friends. The ones I feel sorry for are Kevin Lowe and Mark Messier. Those guys are champions."

The Kings' victory may have knocked the Oilers out of the playoffs, but it also left Gretzky physically and mentally drained. An entire team letdown after the emotional series seemed inevitable, so it wasn't surprising when the Calgary Flames swept Los Angeles in four games in the divisional final, outshooting the Kings by more than 50 shots. Gretzky managed just one goal in the series, but naturally, it made big news. It was his 86th in playoff competition, breaking the record he shared with Mike Bossy.

Despite the disappointing showing against Calgary (which went on to win the Stanley Cup), Wayne was optimistic about the Kings' future. "Maybe we still haven't won anything, but the entire season and victory over the Oilers was a giant step for this organization." And so The Great One went home to his new wife and his new daughter, Paulina, and prepared for another new season; one which would undoubtedly enhance his legend.

13

The Greatest:
Now and Forever?

One measure of Wayne Gretzky's greatness can be gauged by how he's pretty much taken all the drama out of setting records. That The Great One would own most NHL scoring records has been an inevitability since he started methodically breaking single-season marks in 1982. Years from now, hockey fans will not be watching an aging Gretzky struggling up and down ice in a vain quest for a scoring record. They'll be watching him pad statistics that may never be equalled. He's owned the career assist mark since 1988 and will most likely surpass Gordie Howe's all-time NHL record of 801 goals sometime during the 1991–92 season (if not sooner).

But what would an NHL season be without the anticipation of another Gretzky achievement? When the 1989–90 campaign began, Wayne was just 14 points shy of breaking Howe's career-points record of 1850, a number which took the legend 1767 games to achieve. As the Kings prepared to play the Edmonton Oilers on October 15, Gretzky had drawn within one point of his idol in just 779 games.

"People have asked me if there's pressure, but it's not like when I beat [Phil Esposito's record] 76 goals," Gretzky said as the big point drew nearer. "That had to be done in a single year so you didn't know about it for sure. But if I don't break the points record tonight, I'll break it the next game, so everybody should just have fun with it."

Before the season began, Wayne predicted he would break the record during the Kings' first visit to Edmonton. If he couldn't break it in L.A., he reasoned, "it would be fitting" to do it in Edmonton before a sellout crowd of his old fans—and Oilers owner Peter Pocklington in attendance.

As usual, Wayne didn't waste any time. With less than five minutes gone in the first period, Gretzky assisted on a Bernie Nicholls goal to tie Howe. Then, with excitement over the record point filling the arena, the Oilers and Kings proceeded to play a classic hockey game. The teams were tied, 3–3, when with 4:40 remaining in the third period, Glenn Anderson tipped in Kevin Lowe's slap shot, giving Edmonton the lead. Of course, that only set the stage for more Gretzky flourishes. Now he could not only break the record, but tie the game at the same time.

Wayne had been on the ice for almost three minutes when the Kings pulled goaltender Mario Gosselin for a sixth attacker. While his teammates skated frantically around the Oiler goal, Gretzky hovered behind the net waiting for the opportunity to strike. Suddenly, Dave Taylor sent a pass from the right corner in front of the goal. Gretzky bolted from his position, grabbed the puck while moving in front of the net, and backhanded the puck between Oiler goalie Bill Ranford and the post. The clock read: 53 seconds.

As Gretzky leaped into the air and was surrounded by his teammates, the Oiler fans, many of whom had passed a statue of Gretzky on the way into the building, gave him an ovation that lasted two minutes. It must have seemed like old times. The game was stopped for another ten minutes as Gretzky received gifts from the NHL, his former teammate Mark Messier and, of course, Gordie Howe. A few days earlier, Howe had been bitten by the record-setting bug, announcing he would try to be activated for one game—at age 61—after the new year so he could extend his record of playing in five decades to six. "I challenge the little guy [Gretzky] to break that one," Howe joked.

But as is befitting a record-setter, Wayne wasn't through amazing the fans and his teammates. This was now his night and it wouldn't be complete without a Kings victory that he engineered. With one minute and 36 seconds remaining in the five-minute overtime period, Gretzky took control of the puck behind the net (where else?) and, in one motion, whirled out in front and whipped the puck past Ranford. The Great One had added yet another chapter to his legend.

Prior to his breaking Howe's record, someone suggested to Gretzky that if he averaged 150 points over the next seven years, he'd finish his career with around 3000. (A total which would make him number one for points in a *pro* hockey career. *Sports Illustrated* pointed out after Gretzky set the NHL points record that counting World Hockey Association totals, Howe is approximately 400 points ahead of Gretzky.) That prodded Wayne to speculate about which of his records would stand the test of time.

"The 50 goals I got in 39 games will be tough to beat," he said. "So will 92 goals in a season. But I think the toughest will be the 51-game point streak [in 1983–84] and the 163 assists [in 1985–86]. If Mario [Lemieux] stays healthy, I give him a chance to score about 3000, too. He's a real great one."

But not the Greatest One, despite the fact that Lemieux had won the scoring titles in 1988 and '89. All one has to do to end the "Who's Better: Gretzky or Lemieux?" debate that has been raging since the six-foot-four, two hundred-pound center began his career with the Pittsburgh Penguins in 1984 is talk to opposing players, which is what Stan Fischler did for a New York *Daily News* column in mid-October of '89. Out of 20 New York Islanders polled, 13 said they'd rather have Gretzky as a teammate than Lemieux. Three voted for Mario and four abstained.

"Gretzky is unique because so many players feed positively off him," said the Islanders' Patrick Flatley. "Nobody else in the league has the quality of getting 20 other guys so energized by his own play."

"Having played with Gretzky last year," said goaltender Glenn Healy, "I can tell you firsthand he's capable of changing the attitude of any team into a winner. Sure, Lemieux is great with the puck, but, without it, he's not as awesome as Wayne."

And added veteran forward Don Maloney: "If I'm looking to win the Stanley Cup in the next year or two or three, I'd want Wayne on my team. Nobody can match his competitiveness."

Two weeks after Fischler's poll, the Kings went into Pittsburgh and Gretzky played as if he wanted not only to prove the Islanders right, but to silence, once and for all, everyone who had given the slightest thought to Lemieux being the NHL's best player. Playing like a man on a mission as a banner reading "Wayne Who?" was draped above the ice, Gretzky scored two first-period goals a minute apart. Later he added another goal—for his 46th career hat trick—and three assists to lead the Kings' 8–4 victory, while Lemieux was being held without a goal for the ninth time in 12 games. Mario did manage two assists, but in this showdown The Great One of the Kings clearly humbled the player who would be king. Wayne Gretzky had proven once again that he was not just the greatest hockey player right now—he may be the greatest forever.

WAYNE GRETZKY'S CAREER STATISTICS
(As of Nov. 13, 1989)

Season	Club	League	Regular Season					Playoffs				
			GP	G	A	PTS	PIM	GP	G	A	PTS	PIM
1976-77	Peterborough	OHA	3	0	3	3	0	—	—	—	—	—
1977-78 ab	S.S. Marie	OHA	64	70	112	182	14	13	6	20	26	0
1978-79	Indianapolis	WHA	8	3	3	6	0	—	—	—	—	—
cd	Edmonton	WHA	72	43	61	104	19	13	10*	10	20*	0
1979-80 efg	Edmonton	NHL	79	51	86*	137*	21	3	2	1	3	2
1980-81 ehiik	Edmonton	NHL	80	55	109*	164*	28	9	7	14	21	4
1981-82 ehijklm	Edmonton	NHL	80	92*	120*	212*	26	5	5	7	12	8
1982-83 ehijmnoq	Edmonton	NHL	80	71*	125*	196*	59	16	12	26*	38*	4
1983-84 ehimq	Edmonton	NHL	74	87*	118*	205*	39	19	13	22*	35*	12
1984-85 ehimnopqr	Edmonton	NHL	80	73	135*	208*	52	18	17	30*	47*	4
1985-86 ehijkr	Edmonton	NHL	80	52	163*	215*	46	10	8	11	19	2
1986-87 ehimqr	Edmonton	NHL	79	62*	121*	183*	28	21	5	29*	34*	6
1987-88 gnp	Edmonton	NHL	64	40	109*	149	24	19	12	31*	43*	16
1988-89 eg	Los Angeles	NHL	78	54	114	168	26	11	5	17	22	0
1989-90	Los Angeles	NHL	18	10	25	35	22	—	—	—	—	—
NHL TOTALS			792	647	1225	1872	386	131	86	188	274	56
WHA TOTALS			80	46	64	110	19	13	10	10	20	2
PRO TOTALS			872	693	1289	1982	405	144	96	198	294	58

See next page for footnotes.

* Led League
a OHA Second All-Star Team (1978)
b Named OHA's Rookie of the Year (1978)
c WHA Second All-Star Team (1979)
d Named WHA's Rookie of the Year (1979)
e Won Hart Trophy (1980, 1981, 1982, 1983, 1984, 1985, 1986, 1987, 1989)
f Won Lady Byng Trophy (1980)
g NHL Second All-Star Team (1980, 1988)
h NHL First All-Star Team (1981, 1982, 1983, 1984, 1985, 1986, 1987)
i Won Art Ross Trophy (1981, 1982, 1983, 1984, 1985, 1986, 1987)
j NHL record for assists in regular season (1981, 1982, 1983, 1985, 1986)
k NHL record for points in regular season (1981, 1982, 1986)
l NHL record for goals in regular season (1982)
m Won Lester B. Pearson Award (1982, 1983, 1984, 1985, 1987)
n NHL record for assists in one playoff year (1983, 1985, 1988)
o NHL record for points in one playoff year (1983, 1985)
p Won Conn Smythe Trophy (1985, 1988)
q Won Emery Edge Award (1984, 1985, 1987)
r Selected Chrysler-Dodge/NHL Performer of the Year (1985, 1986, 1987)

Obtained from Indianapolis with Eddie Mio and Peter Driscoll for cash, 1978.
Reclaimed by Edmonton as an under-age junior prior to Expansion Draft, June 9, 1979.
Claimed as priority selection by Edmonton, June 9, 1979.

Obtained from Edmonton, August 9, 1988, with Mike Krushelnyski and Marty McSorley for Jimmy Carson, rights to
Martin Gelinas, and Kings 1st round draft picks in 1989, 1991, 1993.

NATIONAL HOCKEY LEAGUE RECORDS HELD OR SHARED BY WAYNE GRETZKY
(As of Nov. 13, 1989)

Career Record

MOST POINTS:
   1872—792 games in eleven seasons, 1979–80 through 1989–Nov. 1990

MOST ASSISTS:
   1225—792 games in eleven seasons, 1979–80 through 1989–Nov. 1990

MOST ASSISTS, INCLUDING PLAYOFFS:
   1413—1225 regular season and 188 in playoffs

MOST ASSISTS, CENTER:
   1200—1979–80 through 1988–89

MOST GAMES SCORING THREE-OR-MORE GOALS:
   46—1979–80 through 1989–Nov. 1990

MOST CONSECUTIVE 40-OR-MORE GOAL SEASONS:
   10—1979–80 through 1988–89

MOST 100-OR-MORE POINT SEASONS:
   10—1979–80 through 1988–89

MOST CONSECUTIVE 100-OR-MORE POINT SEASONS:
   10—1979–80 through 1988–89

HIGHEST GOALS-PER-GAME AVERAGE, CAREER: (300 or more goals)
   .823—637 goals in 774 games

HIGHEST ASSISTS-PER-GAME AVERAGE, CAREER: (500 or more assists)
   1.55—1200 assists in 774 games

HIGHEST POINTS-PER-GAME AVERAGE, CAREER: (900 or more points)
   2.37—1837 points in 774 games

Regular Season

MOST GOALS, ONE SEASON:
   92 in 1981–82

MOST ASSISTS, ONE SEASON:
   163 in 1985–86

MOST POINTS, ONE SEASON:
   215 in 1985–86

MOST GAMES SCORING THREE-OR-MORE GOALS, ONE
   SEASON:
   10 in 1981–82, 1983–84

HIGHEST ASSIST-PER-GAME AVERAGE, ONE SEASON (35 or
   more):
   2.04 in 1985–86

HIGHEST POINTS-PER-GAME AVERAGE, ONE SEASON,
   INCLUDING PLAYOFFS (50 or more): 2.69 in 1985–86

MOST GOALS, ONE SEASON, INCLUDING PLAYOFFS:
   100 in 1983–84

MOST ASSISTS, ONE SEASON, INCLUDING PLAYOFFS:
   174 in 1985–86

MOST POINTS, ONE SEASON, INCLUDING PLAYOFFS:
   255 in 1984–85

MOST GOALS, ONE SEASON, BY A CENTER:
   92 in 1981–82

MOST ASSISTS, ONE SEASON, BY A CENTER:
   163 in 1985–86

MOST POINTS, ONE SEASON, BY A CENTER:
   215 in 1985–86

MOST SHORTHANDED GOALS, ONE SEASON:
   12 in 1983–84

MOST GOALS, MINIMUM 50 GAMES, FROM THE START OF
   THE SEASON:
   61 in 1981–82

LONGEST CONSECUTIVE POINT-SCORING STREAK:
   51 games in 1983–84

LONGEST CONSECUTIVE POINT-SCORING STREAK FROM THE
START OF A SEASON: 51 games—October 5, 1983
through January 4, 1984

LONGEST CONSECUTIVE ASSIST-SCORING STREAK:
17 games—November 26, 1983 through January 4, 1984
(Tied with Paul Coffey, 1985–86)

MOST ASSISTS, ONE GAME:
7—Three times, February 15, 1980; December 11, 1985;
February 14, 1986
(Ties NHL Record)

MOST ASSISTS, ONE ROAD GAME:
7 at Chicago, December 11, 1985 (Ties NHL Record)

MOST ASSISTS, ONE GAME, BY A PLAYER IN HIS FIRST NHL
SEASON:
7 in 1979–80

MOST GOALS, ONE PERIOD:
4 in 1980–81

Stanley Cup Playoff Records

MOST POINTS, CAREER:
274—86 goals, 188 assists in 131 games

MOST CAREER PLAYOFF GOALS:
86 (in 131 games)

MOST CAREER PLAYOFF ASSISTS:
188 (in 131 games)

MOST CAREER THREE-OR-MORE GAMES:
7 (Ties NHL Record)

MOST POINTS, ONE PLAYOFF YEAR:
47—1985 (17 goals, 30 assists)

MOST ASSISTS, ONE PLAYOFF YEAR:
31—1988 (in 19 games)

MOST SHORTHANDED GOALS, ONE PLAYOFF YEAR:
3—1983

MOST POINTS, IN FINAL SERIES:
　　13—1988 vs. Boston, four games, 3 goals and 10 assists
MOST GOALS, IN FINAL SERIES:
　　7—1985 vs. Philadelphia, six games (Ties NHL Record)
MOST ASSISTS IN FINAL SERIES:
　　10—1988 vs. Boston, four games
MOST ASSISTS IN ONE SERIES (OTHER THAN FINAL):
　　14—1985 Conference Final vs. Chicago, six games (Ties
　　NHL Record)
MOST ASSISTS, ONE PLAYOFF GAME:
　　6—1987 Division Semi-Final vs. Los Angeles, April 9
MOST ASSISTS, ONE PERIOD:
　　3—1981, April 8, vs. Montreal
　　　1983, April 24, vs. Chicago
　　　1985, April 25, at Winnipeg
　　　1987, April 9, vs. Los Angeles
　　　1987, April 12, at Los Angeles (All Tie NHL Record)
MOST SHORTHANDED GOALS, ONE PLAYOFF GAME:
　　2—1983 vs. Calgary
　　　1985 vs. Winnipeg (Both Tie NHL Record)
MOST POINTS, ONE PERIOD:
　　4—1987 (1 goal, 3 assists), 3rd period, April 9 vs. Los
　　Angeles (Ties NHL Record)
FASTEST GOAL FROM THE START OF A PERIOD, OTHER THAN
　　THE FIRST:
　　0:09—1983, 2nd period, April 6 vs. Winnipeg (Ties NHL
　　Record)

NHL All-Star Game Records

MOST GOALS, ONE GAME:
　　4—1983 at Uniondale, New York
MOST GOALS, ONE PERIOD:
　　4—1983, 3rd period, at Uniondale, New York
MOST POINTS, ONE PERIOD:
　　4—1983, 3rd period, at Uniondale, New York

NATIONAL HOCKEY LEAGUE—ALL-TIME SCORING LEADERS
(As of Nov. 13, 1989)

Points

		Teams	GP	Points
1.	WAYNE GRETZKY	Edmonton, L.A.	792	1872
2.	Gordie Howe	Det, Hartford	1767	1850
3.	Marcel Dionne	Det, L.A., NYR	1348	1771

Goals

		Teams	GP	Goals
1.	Gordie Howe	Det, Har	1767	801
2.	Marcel Dionne	Det, L.A., NYR	1348	731
3.	Phil Esposito	Chi, Bos, NYR	1282	717
4.	WAYNE GRETZKY	Edmonton, L.A.	792	647
5.	Bobby Hull	Chi, Wpg, Har	1063	610

Assists

		Teams	GP	Assists
1.	WAYNE GRETZKY	Edmonton, L.A.	792	1225
2.	Gordie Howe	Det, Hartford	1767	1049
3.	Marcel Dionne	Det, L.A., NYR	1311	1024

WAYNE GRETZKY'S NATIONAL HOCKEY LEAGUE AWARDS

HART MEMORIAL TROPHY (Regular Season Most Valuable Player)
1980, 1981, 1982, 1983, 1984, 1985, 1986, 1987, 1989

ART ROSS TROPHY (Regular Season Scoring Championship)
1981, 1982, 1983, 1984, 1985, 1986, 1987

CONN SMYTHE TROPHY (Stanley Cup Playoffs Most Valuable Player)
1985, 1988

LESTER B. PEARSON AWARD (NHL's Outstanding Player—
Selected by players)
1982, 1983, 1984, 1985, 1987

LADY BYNG MEMORIAL TROPHY (Most Gentlemanly Player)
1980

EMERY EDGE AWARD (Best Plus-Minus rating)
1984, 1985, 1987

CHRYSLER-DODGE/NHL PERFORMER OF THE YEAR
1985, 1986, 1987